Convergence
Encounters with an Impossible Being

John Coster

Foreword

Somewhere, moving as quietly as a tiny grub burrowing into autumn leaves, a giant glides behind the trees. He shows us his strength when we least expect it. A boulder descends through the air and breaks the calm surface of the water, shattering the mirror, disrupting the image we have of ourselves.

What is love but sharing in the wonder? I am sharing this with you: the unexpected country, the secret landscape right in our own back yard.

I am sitting in the living room of a small, timber-framed house in the Pelham hills about five miles east of Amherst. Dark, hand-hewn beams span the ceiling. A wainscoting of wide pine boards runs around the lowest quarter of the plaster walls, and the floors are of similar wood, as is the mantle above the fireplace, in which sits a large Vermont Castings wood stove. There is a Dutch oven in the brick to the left of the fireplace and below that another chamber. Years ago, the occupants of the house placed hot coals from the fire into the lower chamber to heat the space above for baking bread. The house was built in 1790, the first full year of constitutional government in the United States. George Washington was president. This is the house Donna rented the month before we met.

It has been a beautiful summer. It seems to rain mainly at night! Brilliant, blue-sky days have followed in succession. The road to Donna's takes you high up into the hills. There are some lovely old farms just beyond us and a good view of the Holyoke Range. She's right on the edge of the Cadwell Forest, the home of numerous wild creatures. Her road actually has MOOSE CROSSING signs on it! Very wild yet so close to Amherst. And quiet, very quiet. Tonight I'll be working on the "Box of Letters" project, scanning documents and maybe writing some more. We'll see what tomorrow brings.

The above sections of a letter to my children mark the beginning of my sojourn in the "little house in the forest" around which the following story unfolded. I am a musician, songwriter, and instrumentalist who mixes traditional Celtic-based music with my own songs. I also have an abiding interest in history, a subject I studied as an undergraduate and later on in graduate school.

When I met Donna, I was very involved in researching and writing about a box of family letters written by ancestors who had played a prominent role in the American Revolution. Donna, who had recently completed a master's degree in psychology as well as a year-long intensive course in nutrition, was, like me, fascinated by family history. She had loved renting this little house with its three fireplaces clustered about a central chimney to ward off the cold in an era before woodstoves. Some of our ancestors had actually served together in the War for Independence. Donna's home and our mutual interests seemed to offer the perfect base from which to launch our respective projects, my book and her new practice as a health coach. There we were, brought together synchronistically in a little post-and-beam cottage that had been built during those very years I was writing about. During our first month together, however, something happened that turned our attention from early American history to a very different area of research.

Donna and I became convinced that we were being visited by a gigantic manlike creature, presumably a Sasquatch, if one can ever presume anything about the objectivity of human perceptions or about a being whose very existence is in dispute. There was Donna's initial sighting in the nearby Quabbin watershed forest, described below, followed by sporadic but consistent incidents that accumulated—noises, handprints, and finally, a display of strength that defies all other explanations.

The creatures I knew might inhabit the surrounding woods were exotic enough: fisher cats, the coyote wolf hybrids that are now thriving in New England, and, according to many witnesses, the occasional mountain lion. Moose were common too. I enjoyed knowing that these animals had returned to the forests of their ancestors. Their presence made me feel closer to the lost world of the American frontier, the setting of much of that family history I was discovering. But the being we were now encountering seemed to come from an era much more remote than the American Revolution.

As I imagined him, he emerged from deep mythology, striding out of the Ice Age and a world of giants, passing through the trees in our darkened yard so quietly it seemed he was slipping through time itself.

Of course, I've sometimes wondered about myself, had moments of doubt. Even as I have recorded these events, I have said to myself, "This can't really be happening. We are imagining things, not observing *reality*." Yet, when I look at all the separate incidents, what we've heard and seen, the physical evidence, and similar experiences of others, I know that we've encountered a very real creature. Imaginary beings don't independently appear to unacquainted witnesses or leave footprints in the snow.

I began this journal so that I would have an accurate record of an encounter I thought would be a once-in-a-lifetime event, a strange tale I might someday tell my grandchildren. Perhaps, I'd write a magazine article. I could not have imagined that Donna's sighting that September evening was the beginning of a much longer story. Whenever I assumed that this odd chapter in our lives had concluded, some new incident would startle and distract us.

We are living in a time when many people seem to ignore what they see around them: the altered climate, the disappearing resources and species, the overwhelming changes bearing down upon us. They just go on about their business. Throughout the last year, I've often felt like that as well, just wanting to detach myself from this bizarre experience and shut out the intrusions of this being who has challenged my assumptions about the world and blurred the boundary between imagination and reality. However, again and again, I've been compelled to record some new event and consider what its meaning might be. I can't simply say, "This isn't really happening."

September 2014

On Monday, September 22, I got home at about 4:00 pm and suggested to Donna that we take a walk. It was a beautiful clear day, and we decided to check out a trail in the Quabbin forest that she had walked in the past. We got to the trail gate at a little after 5 and headed out towards the reservoir at the trail's end. Donna noted with some concern that a friendly neighborhood dog that had always greeted her in the past was not around this time, a big genial golden retriever. She wondered if he had died.

The woods were very quiet, and there was no noticeable breeze. It was cool, but a strong sun shone through the trees, illuminating the mixed hardwood forest with the slanted light of late afternoon. We followed the trail down to the water, realizing as we went that this was an old road to the town of Enfield, one of the four towns submerged when the reservoir was filled in 1940. Donna remarked that this road was probably one often taken by her grandfather when, as a young man, he had delivered produce from the Belchertown farm where he worked to the village now submerged in the former valley of the Swift River. Descending between steep banks, the old road brought us out to the shore and the bright but fading sunlight of a perfect fall day, then, marked by the remnants of stone walls, continued down into the depths where the foundations of the little town lie ninety feet below the surface.

The walk down here had been uneventful. We had seen no birds or animals, but there was scat on the trail, mostly coyote it seemed. Certainly, abundant wildlife lived here. We sat on a big boulder, looking out over the water as the blue sky deepened into evening, noting different landmarks in the distance: the tower on a hill above the eastern shore, the tip of the Prescott Peninsula, the Windsor Dam to the south.

The approaching twilight soon made me oddly nervous and I suggested that we head home.

It was a relatively short walk back to the gate, about twenty minutes at a moderate pace, and we still had plenty of daylight. I did notice something unusual, however. The forest was completely silent. I heard no birds and, more significantly, no insects. Typically, the woods this time of year, under such weather conditions, are gently ringing with the late-summer sounds of insects, a kind of subdued whir and jingle that announces the beginning of fall. This high-frequency vibration had vanished; the only sound was that of our own footsteps.

A little past the halfway point in our walk back to the car, Donna turned suddenly and exclaimed, "What the hell was that?!" She was a step or two behind me, and I turned to see her pointing into the woods with a look of astonishment on her face. There was a logged-over area of low brush between us and the forest beyond but fairly good visibility between the trees. I could see nothing but had a strange sense that something was indeed there. I cannot say why this was the case since I had neither seen nor heard anything consciously, but my eyes scanned the forest from our route up the trail to the open area and trees beyond, into which Donna was still pointing. "It was very tall and white, and was moving behind those trees," she said. We both stared into the woods but saw nothing and, in spite of the odd stillness, heard no sounds of movement. Before I could coax a better description out of her, Donna asked me if a moose or some other animal could possibly be partly white and also taller than me (6'3"). I replied that I didn't think so and she said with considerable alarm, "Well, this was white from its head down."

"Head?" I asked.

"Yes, it looked like some guy dressed in that big white alpaca coat with a hood." I had inherited the winter coat from my brother, one with a hood that made me look like some kind of arctic shaman.

It was very warm but kind of silly looking and had evoked jokes about the Abominable Snowman. It was a coat I had sometimes worn to parties on cold winter nights.

Donna continued to struggle for the most rational explanation for what she had seen. Could it have been sunlight striking a birch tree? No, there were no birch trees, and she had seen arms moving and a head, caught further glimpses as it passed behind trees, then briefly, in a clear space between tree trunks, seen the whole body…a very large man, dressed in white, and *walking*. "That's what it must have been," she offered. But why had it come from behind us, then seemed to pace us at a distance, she asked, posing the question to herself as well as to me. She thought she had first glimpsed it out of the corner of her eye coming up quickly, then seen it clearly as it moved more slowly between the tree trunks. "It *must* have been some guy," she reiterated, "but he was very, very tall."

"Way taller than me?" I asked. "Dressed in a white fur coat on the last day of summer, moving silently through the woods?" We looked at each other. Donna had seen some very large man-like creature, something that seemed impossible, unless of course her mind had conjured it out of thin air. I very much doubted this possibility. Donna is keenly observant, a seasoned hiker, and a highly intelligent, analytical thinker.

I pulled a large clasp knife out of my pocket, grabbed her hand, and insisted on moving quickly back to the car. I had a strong sense that some real being was out there, and I suddenly felt a wave of extreme fear. Donna, however, was smiling broadly. She kept slowing down and looking back as if hoping for another glimpse of whatever it was she had seen. My extreme fear, an emotion I cannot easily account for, subsided when we got back to the car. Donna still seemed dazed.

Though I had long suspected that the legendary Sasquatch might be a real creature, I'd never imagined that one would turn up in

Western Massachusetts, or that it might be white. Yet, what Donna described did match reports by other purported Sasquatch witnesses.

Could this *actually* have been what she saw? She had always assumed the subject was just so much tabloid nonsense. I admit I had been interested in stories of Bigfoot since studying evolution and primate behavior back in school; not that my professors believed in the creature, but the whole subject of man and his near relatives has fascinated me, and I've followed the research as it has progressed over the years. Now it is largely agreed that humans evolved in what anthropologist Chris Stringer calls a kind of Tolkien world, where different hominins coexisted for tens of thousands of years. The discovery of the "hobbit people," small hominin called *Homo floresiensis* who supposedly died out only 12,000 years ago, suggests this view of our ancestral past as do other recent finds, the Denisovans and *Homo naledi*.

After we got home, we decided to do a little research. Once Donna relaxed a bit, three possibilities emerged. She had seen a large, white-furred, bipedal, manlike creature; she had seen a very tall man dressed all in white including a hood, who moved with uncanny quiet through the forest and somehow quickly disappeared; or she was experiencing a kind of waking dream or extreme trick of the eye. We decided to dismiss the tall-man-dressed-in-white option. The figure was simply too big and had moved too quickly with too little noise. We Googled "Sasquatch Quabbin Reservoir." Surprisingly, a number of relevant sites came up. The first we looked at was *The Search for Bigfoot at the Quabbin Reservoir*. We were astonished to find here the video of an interview with another hiker who had been only a couple of miles from where we'd just had our encounter, when he had seen what he believed to be a "white Bigfoot." We sat there stunned. It was one thing to entertain the notion that we had seen such a creature, but to so quickly find support for the possibility was a shock. Donna began to cry gently, the way a person cries when overcome with joy or after witnessing some inspiring victory. What was she reacting to? Was she just relieved to know that her vision of the white Sasquatch did not represent some break with external reality? The interviewer did not inspire a lot of confidence. He attributed some large bird tracks to a creature he referred to as "Birdzilla" and filmed himself collecting water samples from a stream and muttering vaguely about taking them "back to the lab." However, the hiker he interviewed seemed like a completely reasonable and sincere fellow. What were the chances of two people unbeknownst to each other seeing the same thing in the same area, if it weren't real?

Further searching led us to another man who had been terrorized by noises outside his house, also only a couple of miles from Donna's sighting—grunts and howls like those on purported Sasquatch recordings from the Northwest. This guy had posted photos on line of very large, five-toed, human-looking footprints in the snow, pictures that his daughter had taken at the Quabbin while on a field trip.

Later that evening, I emailed the administrator of another website we had found, Squatchachusetts.com. There was little on the site in the way of information, but there again were photographs of some very large, bare footprints impressed into snowy ground. I recounted the details of our encounter and received a reply the next morning from Jon Wilk, the site's creator, inviting us to give him a call. I wrote back that I would contact him that evening. Around five o'clock, Donna and I took another walk, this time in the heavily trafficked Quabbin Park. We were not at all inclined to go back to the lonely trail where we'd had our encounter. We both found that prospect downright frightening. From the Enfield Lookout, we surveyed the vast landscape of the reservoir and surrounding hills. The weather was again beautiful. At about six o'clock, just when Donna had seen the tall white figure, I walked into the woods a short way, then called her over. "Listen," I said. The gentle ringing of the insects was an obvious contrast to the silence that had surrounded us the previous evening in a very similar forest.

We spoke with Jon Wilk that night. He was animated, excited by our encounter, and glad to share his extensive knowledge. His own interest, he told us, had begun twenty years before when, as a young forest ranger, he had encountered two hairy, bipedal creatures in the Savoy Forest. He'd been picking up trash at a campsite one night and come upon a smallish one making off with the garbage bag from a trash barrel. It stopped and looked briefly at him while he stood staring in disbelief. Then, a terrifying roar erupted from behind him. He turned to see a giant creature standing, snarling at him from just beyond the back of his pickup truck. He jumped into the cab, his heart racing, his body shaking as he attempted to radio the main ranger station. Then a rock hit the back of the cab and he floored the vehicle to safety. He did not return to that spot for many years. He was so scared that he had himself transferred to another region. His boss had evidently heard enough stories to not think him crazy. In response to Jon's tale, he had pulled out a file full of similar reports, as if to assure him unofficially that he understood.

All these years later, Jon still felt the visceral effects of his encounter. He now was part of a small research group that included one other retired forest ranger and an active state trooper. They have spent countless hours in the forest, recording possible Sasquatch vocalizations and casting and photographing suspected footprints. There have been many more sightings recently, he says—one by an elderly woman, just two weeks before ours. Jon has actually left food out for those creatures and believes they pass through his property on a route that seems to link the Quabbin with the Holyoke Range. He claims that they have left, in return, small seemingly symbolic offerings, such as pebbles and stones.

Sometimes at night, they have banged on the walls of his house. It scares him but not enough to make him quit his research. He has invested in night vision and recording equipment and, with a few other team members, often spends a night in the woods where, he says, they have heard the creatures but not yet seen them.

Though open about what he is doing, Jon claims he has little interest in personal publicity or making money from his research and is concerned about what will happen if too many people start looking for, or worse, hunting for Sasquatch. Perhaps because of the trauma of his own encounter, he seems intent on understanding and being at peace with these creatures. This man certainly seems sincere. Donna and I agreed to lead him to the site of our encounter on the following Saturday, September 27th.

Jon's theory that the nearby Holyoke Range might sometimes harbor a Sasquatch (or more than one) stirred up a memory of Donna's. Two friends of her older daughter had had a very bizarre experience one evening while hiking a trail on the Mt. Tom Range, just across the Connecticut River from the Holyoke Range. The two young men were very familiar with the area; one lived just below the mountain, and both had camped there. To these teenagers, this was a place to go for an impromptu party or hang-out. On the night in question, both boys heard a scream so loud and deep that it scrambled their senses. They fled in terror and stopped frequenting the mountain. No one knew what to make of the story, but the boys were both very shaken by what had happened. In their families and social group, the story lived on as a local legend. Even now, a few years later, the boys stuck to their story and still seemed frightened by the memory of that terrible scream.

A bit more research revealed that a Sasquatch-like creature has been reported in Massachusetts for over a century. On August 23rd, 1895, *The North Adams Transcript* wrote an article about a family of hairy wild men who were terrorizing the area and were seen by numerous witnesses.

(http://www.bigfootencounters.com/creatures/injun_meadow.htm)

They were suspected of stealing livestock and creating other damage. A posse of five hundred armed men, the paper announced, would set out on Sunday to find these terrifying creatures. What happened? Perhaps some archive in the Berkshires holds the answer.

THE NORTH ADAMS DAILY TRANSCRIPT
FRIDAY AFTERNOON, AUGUST 23, 1895.

BUILT LIKE A HORSE.

Wild Man Creates Terror Among Farmers Around Injun Meadow,

He Scares Brutes as Well as Human Beings.

Posse to Organize and Make a Determined Effort at Capture.

WINSTED, Conn., Aug. 22.—The wild man was seen again yesterday by passengers on Dodd's stage, on route to Winsted from Sandisfield, Mass. He was in the same tract of brush as when seen last Saturday by Selectman Smith, which is five miles from here on the old and lonesome highway leading to Colebrook.

The wild man lives in "Injun Meadow," as it is known to the countrymen. He is thought to be one of a family of three wild men seen two years ago. The man seen by Mr. Smith had no clothes, but was covered with hair. The wild man was seen in Canaan mountain a few months ago is thought to be the same person.

Farmers in that section are terrorized and afraid to go out of doors after dark, and the robberies of henneries and mysterious disappearance of calves, lambs, and even Sandisfield and Colebrook farms are

Blamed Upon the Wild Men.

Five hundred men leave here Sunday morning to hunt for the strange character. They will go out in gangs and surround Injun Meadow, and Cobble mountain farmers have given the use of their teams free, while every man of the posse is warned to go armed.

On Saturday, Riley Smith, while coming over the road, stopped to pick a few berries, but no sooner had he commenced to eat than the wild man emerged from the center of a batch of berry bushes. Smith was about scared to death. His dog commenced to whine, and with its tail between its legs sought refuge in Smith's wagon under a pile of blankets.

Mr. Smith described the man as an awful looking sight. He is large in stature and his head is the most conspicuous part of his body, being nearly the size of a horse's head. His teeth resemble those of a horse in size, but are pointed. His hands are extra large.

We met with Jon and two of his fellow researchers, Dax and Dave, at noon on Saturday and drove to the trailhead. It was another beautiful day, but this time we could hear the cries of blue jays and that familiar background ringing sound of insects. To Donna's delight, we were accompanied by the friendly golden retriever she remembered from other years, but at a certain point, the dog stopped abruptly, as if it had run into an invisible barrier, and bounded back up the trail.

We walked to the area of Donna's sighting, discussing our different experiences. Dax said he had seen a Sasquatch twice when he lived in Northern Vermont many years before. One he had seen striding across his yard on a moonlit night. Another, or perhaps the same one, had emerged from the forest one night as he was snowmobiling. As one might imagine, he had gunned the machine and raced for home, seeing over his shoulder that the creature was behind, easily keeping pace till it disappeared again into the dark trees. Dave had never seen one, but was fascinated by the subject and thought he had heard the creatures and seen signs of their presence, including footprints. He seemed to have a thorough knowledge of the various authors who had written about the subject, including those few academically credentialed writers who had dared look into it.

Besides being uplifted, Donna had also been somewhat shaken by her experience and was glad to be walking with a group of supportive, seemingly reasonable people who didn't doubt her account.

We didn't see any obvious signs of the creature but did notice something bizarre. An old dog toy, some kind of furry, chewable squirrel, had been placed high on a branch about twelve feet up in a tree. It had been pushed onto the broken branch, forced over some of the leafy offshoots, and was suspended by a rope loop that was part of the toy. A normal-sized person could have done this by grabbing the lowest cluster of leaves and pulling down the branch above, but this discovery did seem odd. The tree was next to the trail, but we had not noticed the stuffed animal on our walk Monday, and this trail was a little-used route to the lake.

At the location of Donna's sighting, Dave walked out through the brush, then, while we watched, moved behind the trees exactly as the creature had. What she immediately noticed was how much shorter our new friend seemed than whatever had walked behind the same trees the previous Monday. Dave looked to be much, much shorter, maybe two feet or more, and he is about six feet tall. The witness we had seen interviewed Monday night, the fellow who had also encountered a possible white bigfoot in the same area, had also mentioned how extremely tall it was, noting its height relative to the brush and trees through which it walked. Like Donna's creature, it seemed to be at least eight feet tall.

The outing lasted about two hours. Jon wanted to hear the story again while in the location of the actual event. He hoped to gauge distances and see if any other evidence could be found, footprints, freshly broken branches, or scat. He even took a stick and hit it against a tree trunk. Wood knocks are supposed to be a kind of Bigfoot communication. Oddly, there was one knock from out in the forest that seemed like a possible reply, but it was ambiguous and could have been attributed to some other source. We soon headed back to our three cars parked by the trail gate, said our goodbyes, and promised that we'd stay in touch. Jon agreed to inform us of any new discoveries that the group made. We spent the rest of the day hiking in another part of the Quabbin, the northernmost boat launch area, about fifteen miles away.

Somehow, the whole subject of Bigfoot seemed less unnerving now. We paid the parking fee at the boat launch area and walked for two hours on the shoreline. It was a warm, gorgeous day, and the soft ground by the water was full of tracks: moose, deer, and a variety of smaller animals. We were both struck by the abundance of wildlife.

The next day was again a brilliant sunny, very warm, Indian summer day. Honestly, we were a bit tired of the distraction Donna's sighting had created. She was much more at ease with the experience now that she had spent some time with a couple of other witnesses who seemed like perfectly normal people. We spent the morning on a few household chores, then drove to another part of the valley west of the Connecticut River where we planned on doing some rock collecting. The whole Sasquatch episode seemed almost humorous. However much corroborating evidence we had encountered, evidence that left little room for disbelief, the notion that giant hairy hominins were roaming the woods of Western Massachusetts was preposterous. What was going to happen next? Would a nine-foot-tall ape man walk into the UMass Anthropology Department, a mere ten miles from our encounter, and demand a spot in the taxonomy of primates? We found it very helpful to laugh about the week's events, even some of the scarier aspects of our experience. I took that common fear that someone could be staring into your house to an absurd extreme, imagining that perhaps our lives illuminated behind windows at night were the equivalent of television for a Sasquatch.

We pulled off at a familiar parking spot on the road to Ashfield to have a picnic lunch and see what interesting stones might have been washed up by summer rains in the nearby creek. As we were climbing over the guardrail, Donna pointed to the hood of her car and said, with a tone of frustration mixed with curiosity, "I'll be right with you, just as soon as I check out that giant hand print." Visible on the dusty hood of her red CRV was, sure enough, the outline of an extremely large hand. Moreover, the fingers were pointing down towards the front of the car, reaching just over the end of the hood, indicating that whoever or whatever had made the print had placed a right hand on the car from behind. Unless the owner of this appendage was extremely tall, much taller than me, it would have been impossible to place the hand in this position, fingers pointing straight ahead, without leaning awkwardly over the hood of the car.

Could the apparent "print" have been composed of some accidental scuff marks? Unlikely. The ratio of the finger lengths to each other was similar to that of a person's hand. There were four fingers, a thumb, and an elongated palm, looking almost but not quite human. The palm seemed noticeably longer than that of a typical human hand. The finger marks were very long as well though some of their length could have been attributed to the fingers sliding backwards as the palm came to rest on the hood of the car.

We shook our heads. We had planned to drop the whole subject for the afternoon. If this was in fact a Sasquatch hand print, it could only have been made at the trailhead while we were all off at the location of Donna's sighting, unless of course we had had a visitor outside our house. There was no other place the car had been parked that was not surrounded by people or traffic. We were both excited but nervous, and maybe a little intimidated.

We went ahead with our picnic and exploration of the creek bed, determined not to let this latest intrusion alter our enjoyment of the day, but first we took photos of the print. When I strayed out of sight around a bend in the stream, I heard Donna call out. Being alone surrounded by steep wooded hillsides made her uneasy.

That evening, I emailed Jon Wilk an account of what had happened along with a photo. He replied a couple of hours later. "Very cool. Here's one of their prints on the side of my house." Attached was a photo of the print in question. It very much resembled the one on Donna's car with its same long, slightly curved, not-quite-human-looking fingers, elongated palm and less opposable thumb.

October 2014

An email I wrote to Jon the morning of October 21 describes the next chapter of our story of the White Sasquatch:

Hi Jon,

A few nights ago, Donna woke up around 4 AM and decided to go downstairs and read near the wood stove. After she had been there for a while, she heard two distinct knocks on the house next to the door. She later said the sound was identical to the sound made when I rapped my knuckles on the clapboards to the right of the door. For some reason, she was not particularly alarmed. She can't say exactly why. Several minutes later, she heard something scrape across the screen of one of the windows facing the street. At that, she became scared and immediately ran into the kitchen, through the den, and up the stairs. She was afraid that a Sasquatch was standing outside, looking through the upper half of the window where there are no curtains, scraping its fingers loudly on the screen as if to get her attention. Uncharacteristically, she left her snack on the table and raced upstairs by the only route that would take her away from that window, not directly in front of it. There were two distinct scraping sounds in rapid succession as if someone with very strong fingernails had swiped at the screen quickly. I could not make the sound with my own soft nails, but later, when I ran several teeth of one of her plastic hair combs across the screen, she said that it closely mimicked what she had heard. There are no branches anywhere near the windows that could have rubbed against that one in the wind. Moreover, it wasn't particularly windy. As far as the knocking is concerned, pine cones do fall on the roof occasionally, usually knocked off by squirrels, but Donna was adamant that this was a different sound. We had heard no dropping cones in a couple of weeks, and two knocks in succession seems very unlikely if attributed to pine cones falling. The wall is protected by a large overhanging soffit so that even in a heavy wind, a pine cone hitting it is unlikely, and Donna says she is completely certain that the knocking was on the wall, NOT on the roof.

We are both fascinated by all of this, if a bit nervous. I have been reading up on the whole subject. One of the things that stands out to me is the academic community's ridicule in spite of the evidence and a belief by some leading scientists that the Sasquatch is almost certainly a real creature. I have been very surprised to learn that three icons of modern science have taken the subject very seriously: Jane Goodall, George Schaller, and Carleton Coon. I'm sending you below the link to an article by Coon. He passed away some time ago but was a big name back when I studied human evolution to fulfill my science requirement at Harvard. There is a lot you'll find interesting in this article, "Why There Has To Be A Sasquatch.".

Another thing I found of interest recently: Are you aware of the "Bigfoot foot" found in Massachusetts this past February? Two boys discovered what they thought was the decomposing foot of a human body and alerted local police. The medical examiner noted that in addition to its very large size, other features of the foot indicated that it was not human. There was a flurry of newspaper articles and some mention of more testing being done, then as far as I know, no further coverage in the media. Unless the police as well as the two boys were hoaxing the public, a preposterous idea, this might be a huge discovery, what skeptics have been demanding for years. So what happened to the story?

Let us know how you're doing and keep us posted on any new developments.

The next day, Donna noticed four roughly parallel streaks across the dust on both the screen and the storm window above. In each case they ran across the entire width of the surface. When I had run my nails across the screen, it had been lower down and I could only scratch at a small section since the metal mesh hurt my nails. Neither the plastic comb nor my hand had made the streaks. The streaks were, however, spaced as one would expect if a large hand with extremely strong nails had been run firmly across the surface at a height greater than would have been natural, even for a very tall man.

October 25

We have had no further evidence suggestive of a visit, but in reflecting on this time at our little house in the forest, one memory stands out. One night in early August, we woke to a very strange noise, an almost plaintive moan of descending pitch, somewhat like the culminating phase of a wolf's howl. It was a much deeper sound than coyotes make and lacked the initial rise in volume and pitch that one usually hears when any kind of canine howls. Moreover, some of its tonality was like that of a low flute, a kind of deep whistling. We listened to recordings of wolves and different species of owls and eventually decided that we might well have heard a wolf. Parts of a wolf's howl seemed to most closely approximate what we heard. People have reported seeing wolves here occasionally, and one was shot by a farmer several years ago and positively identified by biologists at UMass. Also, the eastern coyotes, or coywolves, as some now called them, had blurred the line between the formerly separate species. However, the sound was not really like anything either of us had ever heard before.

Since our encounter, we have wondered if there might not be another explanation for these sounds. Some supposed Bigfoot recordings on the web are similar. Donna heard it once while I was asleep, then woke me. We heard the noise again twice. In my further reading, I was somewhat disconcerted by the 1840 account by a missionary (quoted by Jeff Meldrum) who reported that the Spokane Indians believed that nocturnal Sasquatch visits were often announced by three of its distinctive whistles in succession.

In the past five and a half weeks, Donna and I have felt compelled to look more deeply into the subject of this mysterious creature that has so distracted us. Neither of us has any doubt of its existence. I did not see it, she did, but we discovered the giant hand print together and have seen the photograph of the print on Jon's Wilk's nearby house. How does one account for the similarity between the prints, the five digits similarly proportioned to those on a human hand except by the presence of a large non-human primate? We have also discovered on the web many other witnesses from this very region whose reports corroborate our own experience. Over this same period, we have become more aware of the growing public interest in the subject, capitalized on by such TV programs as "Finding Bigfoot" and "Monster Quest." Amid all the attendant sensationalism and dubious accounts, there is a solid core of credible witnesses, photos, and videos that cannot easily be dismissed. Moreover, as documented by Jeff Meldrum, professor of anatomy and anthropology at Idaho State University in his book *Sasquatch, Legend Meets Science*, the majority of scientists who have studied the evidence seriously do *not* dismiss the idea that a real creature exists. Indeed, they cannot explain the anatomically precise foot and body prints, hair samples, photos, and videos as anything other than evidence of a real being. Certainly a vast conspiracy of hoaxers, combining detailed knowledge of primate morphology and locomotion with the most advanced special effects of Hollywood, randomly popping up in a variety of remote locations and leaving elaborately fabricated evidence where no one is likely to see it, is not a plausible explanation.

What emerges from all of this is an extraordinary conclusion: A very large bipedal primate, possibly a relic hominin, one whose features suggest some fairly close connection to *Homo sapiens*, is roaming the forests in much of North America. As Sherlock Holmes said, "When forced to choose between the impossible and the implausible, we must choose the implausible."

This conclusion, however, only deepens the mystery. How could this creature have existed as it apparently has, surviving in harsh environments and eluding humans, year after year? What combination of intelligence and physical stamina has allowed this to happen? How close to humankind is this "wild man of the woods," and what does his existence tell us about ourselves and our place in nature? And one more question haunts me. Why, in spite of the seriousness with which some eminent scientists view the evidence, is the subject greeted by much of the academic community and other elements of officialdom with a scornful snicker? How ironic that disbelief in Bigfoot may actually represent a society's retreat from the scientific exploration of the world, the exact opposite of the attitude such skepticism is intended to demonstrate.

Both Donna and I feel changed by these last few weeks. We have admittedly been somewhat scared. She will not hike by herself in many areas anymore. I cannot help noticing the similarity between a Sasquatch and some of the scarier creatures of myth: ogres, nightwalkers, and goblins, so many of which are characterized by their almost human features. Indeed, it is precisely the half-human aspect that is at once so alarming and so fascinating. I note the uncanny resemblance between the monster Grendel in *Beowulf* and descriptions of Bigfoot: his great strength, his hairy enormous body, and his nocturnal habits. It is easy to imagine encounters in Europe long ago contributing to Anglo Saxon and Scandinavian folklore.

Stories of "wild men" are found all over the globe, particularly in remote regions. Native Americans of many regions described the creature, depicting it in art and story as they did all the animals in their environment and asserting its reality. They did sometimes fear this being and, in some instances, attributed the disappearance of warriors to the creature and believed that it would sometimes abduct women. But they also often saw the Sasquatch as an "elder brother," much closer to themselves than were any of the other animals. Some tribes thought this elder brother had psychic powers and actually chose to whom it would reveal itself. They sometimes saw it as a guardian of the earth, a being who would appear in times of danger and dislocation as a warning to humans.

Our series of encounters, alarming as it has been, has felt like a blessing, a message of hope. Maybe this is because this creature, whatever it may be, seems to exist on its own terms, unfettered by the constraints of modern society.

November 2014

November 5

Yesterday, after I came home from Amherst, Donna said she really needed to take a walk. I guessed before she said so that she wanted to return to the area of her sighting of the White Sasquatch. We had not been there since our outing with the local investigators on the Saturday after our encounter. The fear we both had experienced had subsided over time. We were nervous, yes, but somehow knew we should go back nonetheless. Donna said she thought there might be some tracks on one of the old roads that led to the location or perhaps some other sign of the creature. She seemed to be searching for corroboration of her experience, or even some form of communication. We had jokingly discussed her relationship with "Squatchy," as she liked to call him. I say "him" because, for no logical reason, we had conferred a gender on the creature as well as the benevolent disposition that "he" had arguably displayed by showing himself to her in the first place with no signs of aggression or mal-intent. We acknowledged this impression as an amusing and comforting fantasy, but the apparently friendly scratching at the screen and somewhat plaintive whistle or moan we had heard outside that August night did seem to suggest that the fantasy might have a basis in fact. We agreed that attributing these human emotions to the being was intellectually silly and not supported by any verifiable evidence, but we enjoyed the notion and could not rule out anything categorically. I figured that seeing a Sasquatch twice in the same spot was about as likely as being struck by lightning twice in the same week, and moreover, I could allay my trepidation with the thought that the creatures almost always seemed to melt quietly into the forest when encountering human beings. We were both fascinated by our apparent encounter with this mythic being. Maybe "enthralled" better describes our condition.

Donna wanted to walk down a trail from another gate that led to where we had been that evening in September. We parked at the entrance and proceeded as planned down this old road, a remnant from the days when the towns under the reservoir were still active communities. About midway down the mile walk to the intersection where the trail meets the path we had followed in September, Donna said she felt as if a Squatch was somewhere nearby. It is her habit to note her feelings and intuitions, cataloging them as she would an observation of any natural phenomenon, without judging them. We saw nothing unusual on our walk down this new trail. After we came to the intersection, Donna took a call from her son. We paused for a while where a power line crosses the trail so they could talk. Then we continued on down to the water and enjoyed the late fall's subdued colors, the reddish brown glow on the hills across the water. We started back when we knew there was only about an hour left till sunset.

As we came to the power line where we had previously stopped, we both noticed a bad smell. It was the kind you associate with a rotting carcass. This was odd because the day was not windy and we had not noticed the smell before, even though we had lingered at this very spot while Donna and her son talked. If a dead deer or some other carrion was in the area, why had the smell not been there less than an hour before? In retrospect, I can't help wondering if this experience is another example of the terrible stench often attributed to Sasquatch. But, of course, it's most likely that a dead animal was the source of the bad odor and that some imperceptible shifting of the breeze was responsible for our noticing it only on our return. However, a few minutes later, something else happened.

As we headed back up the trail to the car, Donna fell behind, then stopped and stared into the forest to our right. When I looked back, she again remarked that she felt as if the creature were near.

Then she shrugged and started to catch up with me. Suddenly, we heard a loud whistle, a sound such as a very adept human whistler might make when calling a dog or getting someone's attention. I expected to see another hiker or perhaps hear some dog bounding through the brush. I looked at Donna and suggested that it was probably just some guy whistling for his dog. The woods were still. "Dogs aren't allowed in the Quabbin," she said with a knowing look. Then the whistling erupted again. It was coming from the brushy forest to our right, a throaty ascending sound that I could not imagine coming from any creature but some rare bird.

Now there was a slight rustling in the underbrush up ahead; it was a flock of wild turkeys quickly crossing the trail from right to left, away from the source of the sound. The whistling happened once more, reminding me of jungle noises I have heard in films set in tropical forests. It was one of the loudest whistles I have ever heard. It was not like the sound of a hawk or any other creature I have encountered in these forests. There was no detectable movement in the brush or sound of leaves being stepped on. The retreating turkeys were now out of earshot and the woods were quiet again.

I tried to convince myself that there had to be some type of bird off in the brush, maybe a migrant passing through from some other region. Donna did not agree, and thinking back, I cannot imagine any bird making such a loud sound, a sound more like the amplified whistle of a football referee than any bird call, though smoother and lacking the trill of an artificial whistle.

Back home that night, I searched vainly among bird calls for a similar whistle. I queried on a birders' site. The closest was a quail's whistle, but this was not really a match. Then on the site "Before It's News," I found that a researcher named Jim Sherman had posted some purported Bigfoot recordings (http://beforeitsnews.com/paranormal/2014/10/listen-to-these-sasquatch-whistle-and-shriek-video-2477030.html). Not only was the whistle he recorded pretty much identical to what we had heard earlier that day, but a second sound was by far the closest approximation to the noise we had heard outside our window in August. Maybe we had again been close to the creature after all.

November 15

A few days ago, Donna noticed some scratches on the hood of her car. She was irritated, thinking that someone had slid something abrasive over the surface, marring the paint with little parallel streaks. When I went out with her to check, I saw immediately what she meant. It looked as if someone had used a wire brush on a small area of the hood. Neither of us has any idea how it had happened, but I don't imagine this has any connection to "Squatchy." I mention the scratched hood only because as we were examining the marks, we suddenly noticed another hand print, smaller and less distinct than the previous one, but still much bigger than a human's and exhibiting the same relatively longer palm. We were both a bit blasé, not really surprised or all that interested. I felt somewhat resigned, as if whatever was going on with these visitations had to be shelved for the time being so I could deal with a number of pressing problems. We went for a walk, and after we returned, I decided I'd photograph the print, but the light had changed and I couldn't see it, though I knew exactly where it had been. The next morning, I looked again but could see no trace of it.

The following day, when I came back from town, Donna had another incident to relate, though she did not mention it till we had talked about many of the day's mundane events. She had spent the afternoon reading several scientific articles about nutrition and psychology. At some point, she'd glanced up and noticed the reflection on the TV screen. The television faces a window on the opposite side of the living room, the side facing the front yard and street. At certain times of day, the window and whatever scene it looks out on is reflected clearly. She saw a tall brown figure walking quickly past the window, which turned and looked at her, seemingly in an open, friendly manner. She immediately jumped up and rushed to the window but could see no one. She crossed to the side window that faced the direction in which the figure had been moving. Still no one. The figure looked just like a brown Sasquatch, tall, hairy, with a domed head, broad shoulders, and the dark skin of the human-like face. She has no idea what to make of this experience. She does not think a Sasquatch could be walking down the street in broad daylight, nor can she quite believe that what she saw on the screen was a distorted image of a man outside, though she finds this the most plausible explanation.

We did search around last night on the web and found a number of similar accounts about the Sasquatch's ability to appear suddenly and then vanish. Strange stuff indeed. But still, so much of the folklore and evidence shows primate characteristics found in some great apes that I really cannot believe these mysterious creatures are anything but flesh and blood. Besides, many large creatures such as the moose in our neighborhood are reclusive, too, and rarely seen.

The following morning, Donna asked me to walk past the house to see how my reflection compared to what she had seen the day before. What we learned was that it was obvious that the figure reflected in the TV screen must have been in the backyard of the house across the street and not on the road itself. This would have accounted for its disappearance, since it could simply have walked behind that house. In that direction it would have only had to cross the next road before entering one of the very large tracts of nearby forest. It would not have had to pass near any other houses. Indeed, it could have walked through nothing but woods before crossing Route 202 several miles away and entering the protected area of the Quabbin watershed. This particular "sighting" remains ambiguous. Could Donna have seen a man with a hood, dressed all in brown? Perhaps. The reflected image was nowhere near as clear as the white creature she had seen walking between trees.

November 17

I had gone upstairs to read while Donna remained by the wood stove talking to her daughter on the phone. After some time, she came upstairs hurriedly and, seeing that I was still awake, asked me if I had heard anything. She had heard a strange screaming coming from out in the woods, loud enough to not have been masked by the tightly sealed windows that faced in that direction. I had heard nothing, but a small electric heater with a fan was on in the upstairs bedroom, and there were no windows facing the forest. The screaming had stopped, but she was alarmed enough to worry that some person, some woman I should say, was in trouble. The cries had been high pitched and very human sounding. Could the noise have come from coyotes or a fisher cat? Perhaps, but it really did not seem to her like a sound from one of those creatures. Once again, recordings on the web of purported Sasquatch screams were the best match. Here was another ambiguous experience.

November 28

We took a walk up the road at about 3 PM to check out the neighborhood after the early snowstorm that had left us without power for Thanksgiving. Just a few hundred yards into our walk, we heard another strange sound, again coming from the woods on the western side of the road. I would describe this sound as a kind of wailing moan, closer to the baying of a hound than a typical coyote howl. The pitch did seem to rise to a fairly high register a couple of times. I thought it might have been some hound dog complaining about being chained up somewhere, but over the few minutes, the eerie wailing seemed to move further away, as if the creature making the sound was moving north along the forested ridge to the west of our road. We both agree this was a very unusual noise but can say little more, other than to note that since living here by the Cadwell Forest, we have heard sounds that are unfamiliar and very difficult to describe. I pulled out my iPhone, hoping I might be able to record what we heard, but the phone was completely dead. No surprise. We had been snowed in without power for almost two days.

December 2014

December 4

This afternoon at about 4:30, I got back from town after a tedious few hours of trying to find the right parts for some new gutters I am installing. Donna had not left the house. She had finally determined how she would approach her book. It seems she will "come out of the Bigfoot closet." She is tentatively calling the book *Lessons from the Sasquatch*. How exactly this whole experience with the creature will figure into a discussion of how big pharma and agriculture are threatening our health is not exactly mapped out. I suppose the appearance of so close a relative to humans in such unlikely and largely secret proximity to modern civilization overturns many assumptions about our world, much as the growing understanding of nutrition and biochemistry threatens what passes for conventional wisdom about health.

At any rate, she had written for hours and had for the first time come to peace with revealing her experience; indeed, she felt that it was important to do so. However, there was a problem. It seemed that her work had somehow not been saved and that the whole afternoon of writing had disappeared down the digital rabbit hole. We both went to work on the problem and finally found to our relief that we could retrieve the file. She had for a while wondered if the seeming loss of her work was some kind warning that she was on the wrong course and would likely elicit nothing but groans and raised eyebrows from her peers at The Institute for Integrative Nutrition. So saving her work was a sign that she should forge ahead. Donna decided to be really sure – to print out what she'd written so far, so she began to set up her printer.

Satisfied that the crisis was over, I grabbed the log tote and headed for the woodshed, deeming it a good time to light a fire in the wood stove. Before reaching the shed, I stopped at my car to grab a headlamp. Even with the moon rising in a clear sky, it would be hard to pick a good assortment of logs without a flashlight. Just as I opened the car door, a loud whistling erupted from the forest. I call it a whistling, but it was a deeper sound than that word suggests, a variation on the other weird noises we had heard, but nearby, maybe fifty yards into the woods. Immediately after came another sound, an ascending whoop, like something I might expect from a giant howler monkey. I dropped my tote and, without shutting the car door, rushed back to the house, feeling somewhat shaken though excited and wanting to tell Donna.

Like all the recent noises, these odd sounds had come from the forest to the west, but this had been much closer than the others; it had actually felt as if it had been projected *at* me. I use the word "felt" advisedly; the sound was one I seemed to feel as well as hear, a vibration that ran up my spine. It reminded me of the whistling we had heard at the Quabbin, but it was deep enough to not even remotely suggest the call of a bird. It was loud and forceful and full of directed intention. I quickly walked upstairs to tell Donna what had happened. She smiled broadly, knowingly. Of course, the file had been saved and printed out. We would both continue to ponder the message of the Sasquatch.

Yesterday evening, we watched a few of the more recent Squatch videos, most of which really seem authentic. I found myself thinking about this whole experience when I woke once during the night. Periodically, the reality of what has happened reasserts itself emotionally. I accept intellectually that these beings must exist; there is too much evidence for any other conclusion, however mysterious their ability to elude people, to disappear so quickly and silently. Nevertheless, I often relegate the creature to a realm of quasi-reality. Sometimes, however, as was the case while watching those videos, the whole subject has a much greater impact on me. I do not think this intermittent fascination made me imagine what I heard tonight. The sound was very real, overpowering actually, and yet so strange it is hard to describe or even to recreate in my mind. I was stunned by what I heard. Still, I am curious about the odd convergence of these inner and outer worlds. Did my fascination with the subject, reanimated over the last two days, somehow call the experience to me, attract the attention of the creature?

December 5

   After I wrote the entry above, we went upstairs to turn in. I was washing up in the bathroom when I thought I heard the sound starting up again outside. In the bathroom, there is a small window that such a sound could penetrate. I rushed into the bedroom to tell Donna to come and check out what I was hearing. But the sound got louder; it was coming from her computer speakers. She was listening to purported Bigfoot recordings from Cliff Barackman of the "Finding Bigfoot" cast. That was the sound I had heard.

http://undebunkingbigfoot.blogspot.com/2013/12/what-kinds-of-sounds-do-sasquatch-make.html

   These sounds are unlike those of any known animal in the forests of Western Mass. I have listened to every species' vocalizations and to all the recordings of birds at the Cornell Lab of Ornithology, particularly the owls. Nothing comes close but these purported recordings of Bigfoot.

   In looking for sounds, we came across several recordings of supposed Bigfoot "speech," as well. The earliest were made by Al Berry and Ron Morehead in the early 1970s in the Sierra Nevadas. I first thought they had to be fakes. Now, listening to very similar "Sasquatch recordings" from Sasquatch Ontario and hearing Scott

Nelson, retired US Navy linguist, state that he believes the Berry-Morehead tapes to be authentic, I am beginning to think that maybe these beings do have a language and, at least in the case of the Ontario recordings, may actually be attempting to communicate with us. What an outlandish idea! What are they really? An offshoot of *Gigantopithecus*, the known giant primate known from the fossil record? Some branch of our family tree more closely connected to *Homo erectus*, a hominin that died off long before humans spread throughout North America? Again, I am struck by how ridiculous this all seems. At 5:30 in the evening, I am startled by the cries of a creature as fantastic as a unicorn, a being I associate with the myths of distant, inaccessible mountains – the Rockies or the Himalayas. At 6:30, I'm wandering around in a modern shopping center, looking bemusedly at trashy magazines about Hollywood divorces and "reality TV." Donna tells me I am acting dazed and confused. Meanwhile, a scant six or seven miles away from the forests around our house, 20,000 university students and faculty go about the business of describing the known world.

December 6

Once again, we choose to explore Squatch stories on the web rather than watch a TV show or just read, and returning to Sasquatch Ontario, we find another curious corroboration of our own experience. We have noted that the hood of Donna's car retained a slight discoloration where the hand print had been, as if some kind of skin oil had altered slightly the paint itself. That discoloration survives even now. In a video interview with Chris Munch, producer of the movie *Letters From the Big Man*, we find mention of the same phenomenon, a seeming oily residue which leaves a mark long after the print has disappeared. At the location in Ontario where Mike Paterson is supposedly involved with habituation and communicating with these beings, they regularly leave marks on vehicles, another form of contact. Our own experience of the hand prints and discoloration lends credence to what Paterson is saying and makes his recordings of Sasquatch speech seem less likely to be fake.

Again and again, we have had experiences, then learned that they are typical of those of others who are encountering Sasquatch. Looking at a web page about another "habituation site," a place where some kind of communication seems to be happening between humans and these creatures, this one in northern Vermont where Christopher Noël reports various subtle forms of communication, piles of rocks, wall knocks, etc., we encounter another odd coincidence. Noël finds a stuffed animal placed up in the crotch of a tree, a reminder of the dog toy we found hung about twelve feet up in that trailside tree at the Quabbin.

Supposed tree structures are another example. On that very ridge from where strange cries seemed to come on the day after Thanksgiving, we find a bizarre formation. Large branches and small uprooted dead trees have been leaned up against both sides of a fallen oak that long ago crashed into the crotch of another tree, where it remains suspended at about a forty-five-degree angle above the ground. The resulting structure looks like a large triangular tent frame. None of the branches or saplings that comprise the frame shows any cut marks. None was sawed or chopped; they were broken off or pulled from the ground. It is very odd, something one might attribute to the imagination of young children were it not too large to be made by seven- or eight-year-olds. On the other hand, it seems too primitive and useless to be some teenager's project. Donna discovered this structure before she imagined any Sasquatch could be roaming in the neighborhood, before she thought such a being could be real. Such structures are commonly thought by believers to be the work of Sasquatch. Pictures of them appear frequently on websites about Bigfoot.

There are still moments when my own sense of what in all of this is real flickers uncertainly. I have not seen anything myself except for those very large hand prints. But I know those strange whistling cries I heard last night were real, as was the shrill whistling we heard at the Quabbin and that sound in the back yard last August. These sounds are so unlike anything I've heard before that it is very difficult to describe them. They combine the throaty qualities of a moan with the flute-like breathiness of a whistle; it cannot be mere coincidence that Native American depictions of the Sasquatch almost always show the creature's lips pursed as if whistling. And how can we dismiss the various recordings now on the web of just such sounds, recordings made in close proximity of various Bigfoot signs and not attributable to any known species? Something very strange is happening, something more than the discovery of a very rare but entirely possible animal. How could such a large creature remain so elusive? Is its secrecy an artifact of culture, something more refined and intentional than a mere instinct to remain hidden? This is the great mystery. Maybe the Sasquatch really are a "people" as the Native Americans used to say and Mike Paterson believes, creatures with families and names and access to worlds and abilities we can barely imagine. Maybe their appearance, as they also claimed, proclaims a time of danger and necessary change, a time when reinvesting the world with wonder is a matter of survival itself.

January 2015

January 6

No more experiences to report since my last entry. Occasionally, I'll check out the latest Squatch videos on YouTube or ferret out some interesting reports, but the whole phenomenon/experience seems to have receded. A friend did post an interesting iPhone video from Maine showing a supposed Sasquatch crossing what looks to be a logging road, and I couldn't resist a humorous comment: "Those Mainers are tough, but they usually wear clothes in winter and have less body hair." Another friend posted the following skeptical and rather lame response: "Folks, to an experienced photographer and his wife, even more experienced, that is an image of dust on the lens cover. I've lived close to the woods in Upstate NY and New England. I've encountered moose and other large critters like bear. I would love to sit down and share some stories with an Abominable, but he doesn't exist. Wait, wait! I have to grab my iPhone and take pictures of that UFO-er-thing!!!"

For the record, I feel pretty certain that this particular video is a hoax. It looks like a man dressed in a costume that is slightly too large and loose. However, calling it an "image of dust" is absurd. Here it is:

http://bigfootevidence.blogspot.com/2015/01/the-maine-bigfoot-footage-clearly-shows.html

It is fascinating to note what people will see or not see depending on their belief system. I don't know why I couldn't resist jumping into the fray somewhat. Maybe I'm addicted to debate.

"Actually, Steven, they do exist. I was hoping to introduce one to the UMass Anthropology Department (only a short walk away for a Sasquatch, considering their stride), but all they'll do is whistle loudly at me from the underbrush, then slip into the forest. All joking aside, a number of the world's most prominent naturalists, though stopping short of a definitive statement, believe the creature's existence is almost certain. The list includes Jane Goodall, George Schaller, and Carleton Coon, a prominent figure at Harvard where I studied primatology back shortly after the last ice age. Encounters have been reported for centuries by diverse peoples, including most Native American tribes. The recent proliferation of videos is simply a result of the new smartphone technology.

Sure, some are fakes, but certainly not all. For an overview of the actual science, look at Dr. Jeff Meldrum's book *Sasquatch: Legend Meets Science*. The subject is quite mysterious, but an international hoax by the world's leading primatologists and hundreds of field workers with a capacity to replicate the bio-dynamically correct footprints of a very large creature in thousands of random remote and scattered locations is not a real possibility. Of course I'm only saying this in hopes that government agents concerned about dissident thinking will leave me alone, secure in the notion that I may be dismissed as a 'Bigfoot believer.' Cheers."

February 2015

February 22

Nothing much to report in the way of new experiences. However, I did get an email from Jon, asking if there had been any activity recently. There has not been, but his inquiry did get us thinking a bit, as did a book Donna discovered, *The Locals*, by Thom Powell. The book is well written and considers all of the wilder aspects of the phenomenon, without ever straying beyond the bounds of rational inquiry. Powell's website picks up where the book left off in 2003.

Perhaps the most astonishing development he reports are recent genetic tests completed by Melba Ketchum. The 109 hair and tissue samples used for the study appear to have produced a conclusion that is mind boggling if soundly based. The creature's genetic makeup is part human, that part which derives from the female component, and part something totally unknown. Checking further into Ketchum's claims on line, I find that she believes her tests reveal the presence of a hybrid, part human and part some unknown creature, a hominin presumably. Hence at some point, she speculates about 15,000 years ago, a female human bred successfully with this unknown being. I don't have the background to understand these results in any detail. Are these tests some kind of fraud, misinterpreted data, or what? What unknown relative of man played Adam to the race of Sasquatch? Do others of his kind still exist or did they until recently?

In talking with Donna and reviewing our experience, I have recalled two incidents that I did not report before. On one of the first nights I spent here, she showed me the back yard, an area that extends past an old garden and abandoned above-ground pool out to the edge of the forest about a hundred yards away. It was a beautiful starry night, dark because there was no moon, but warm and lovely. As we stood looking up at the clear sky above the trees, I became very uneasy; actually, I was quite scared. I have walked along country roads on summer evenings since I was a boy, camped out in the woods many times, too, and never felt like that. I had no reason to suspect there could be anything dangerous in those woods a scant few miles from town in a relatively upscale neighborhood. Sure, the occasional moose or bear could show up, but this is not a frightening prospect. That night, though, for no discernible reason, I became very uncomfortable standing so close to the edge of the dark forest. A sense of panic rose up in me that I awkwardly tried to disguise. I remember my relief as we entered the kitchen from the back yard and I latched the screen door behind me.

On another night, later in the same week, as we stood by the open back door, we heard a strange whirring noise like that of some powerful engine. It seemed to be coming from just above the trees. It was fairly constant for quite a few seconds, then built to a kind of whooshing roar and suddenly stopped, leaving no retreating engine noise or other sound in its wake. I attributed the sound to one of the military cargo planes, the C5s that train in the area, though come to think about it, I've never heard them so low and so late at night. I suppose that's still the most logical explanation. However, a very realistic-looking video on YouTube purporting to show a UFO, a disc on the ground, which takes off from some field, in Germany I believe, captured a sound just like the sound we heard that night. It was shortly after these events that we heard in the back yard the odd whistling howl that I could not identify. I'm writing this down now, wanting to preserve without judgment all the elements of this strange experience. I don't know why I had that feeling of dread, and I'm certainly not claiming there was a UFO hovering over the forest.

February 28

I didn't expect to write further in this journal today, but something of note did happen. We decided to take a hike, this being the first day with temperatures above freezing in a long time. The snow was too deep to consider any of our normal trails without snowshoes, but after driving about for a bit, we noticed that Gate 29 had some cars parked at the entrance and seemed to have been plowed out. Indeed, the gate, new for us, led to an old roadway that was still intact, one of the early paved roads in the region, no doubt. The entire surface had been cleared of all but the last six inches of snow by watershed crews and was ideal for hiking or cross country skiing. We passed several hikers and one skier as we marched along the wide swath of road cutting through the forest. After about an hour, we realized we'd have to turn back if we wanted to get to the car before dark, so we stopped some indeterminate distance short of the shoreline. We couldn't tell whether the lake was a mile ahead or just around the next bend, but we did not want to face a long walk in the dark.

As we approached a part of the road intersected by another broad power line, we heard several distinct and very loud metallic-sounding knocks, like a sledgehammer striking some kind of resonant metal surface, like a pipe or steel girder. The sound had come from up ahead on the trail and to our left. Sure enough, in that direction the metal towers of the power line were staggered over the cleared ground, spaced about every hundred yards to support the wires that stretched up over the ridge to the west of the roadway. Donna wondered if someone could have been striking some part of these steel towers. Indeed, the sound did seem to come from their location, and there were no houses nearby where someone might have been banging on metal. She wondered if a Squatch could substitute a tower for a tree: tower knocking instead of tree knocking. When we got home, what did she find online but an article about Sasquatches using power lines as convenient pathways and banging on the towers to communicate over longer distances than would be possible with simple tree knocks? What to make of this? Who knows? There were towers just where that sound seemed to have originated and no signs that people had been there, no tracks from the roadway leading in that direction, and the snow was about three feet deep.

March 2015

March 6

Today at about 4 PM, I walked into the Cadwell Forest on the main trail. It had been compacted by snowmobiles and skiers and was easy walking. Donna was visiting her daughter and I needed some air and exercise. The same barred owl I had been hearing every evening in that direction, or another of his kind, was loudly hooting even though the sun was still bright in the brilliant blue sky. Maybe three-quarters of a mile into the forest, I noticed some strange tracks, deep but somewhat filled in from the recent small storms that have followed the bigger ones. They looked like the tracks of a very large person proceeding in a right-left sequence, but it was impossible to tell what their exact size had been or what details they might have at first revealed. They had certainly been made after the last big storm but did not show the shape or shallow depth of snowshoes. They came up to the packed trail and resumed again in the deep snow on the other side, ascending through the trees. They were much larger than my own tracks, but after such wild weather there was no way to measure them accurately. What really impressed me was the length of the stride. I wanted to see how my own steps would compare, but when I attempted to position myself so that I could walk alongside the mysterious impressions, I sank deeper than my knees and actually fell over. Whatever had made these tracks had not dragged its feet through the upper levels of the snow, as was necessary for me, but had placed its feet down and pulled them up and over. There was no depression of any kind between the tracks such as a creature would have to make when plowing along or kicking its way through the drifts. The distance between steps looked to be over five feet. I put my glove down next to the nearest track to use as a reference and took some pictures.

When I got home I measured the glove at 9½ inches. I adjusted the size of the picture on my iPhone till the glove on my screen measured ¼ inch and the space between the tracks 1¾. This made the distance about sixty-five inches from the back of one print to the heel of the next, about double my own normal stride. I wondered if a moose could have done this. Their legs are long, but I've seen them kick their way through deep snow, and if they were to lift their legs high over the surface, I would imagine the tracks would not have the general contours of a human foot. Of course, I wonder if this has anything to do with the usual suspects. Maybe I can find someone more familiar with the appearance of tracks in such deep snow. I would have followed the trail, but without snowshoes the woods are still almost impassable. Moreover, the prints went up over rough rocky terrain, away from any path.

March 7

Donna and I went back out the Cadwell Forest trail to reexamine the tracks I had found. Somehow, I managed to walk right past them and continue about a half mile further up the trail. We came to a higher elevation where the trail bends south through a predominantly birch forest, a place I had not reached the previous day. I was perplexed. How had I missed what I was looking for? I must have misjudged how far off the road the tracks were and how long I had walked before I found them. We turned back, not fretting about my disorientation, but enjoying the beautiful weather here in the waning days of a memorable winter.

As we returned down the trail, we noted some of the other tracks in the snow: deer tracks, much narrower with long grooves where the deer's legs had kicked through the surface, wider pathways where some creature's body had plowed along. With the snow at three feet and more, most animals could not make their way without breaking the surface; they simply would not be tall enough to march along, leaving the space between steps undisturbed. A coyote or fox, I suppose, could bound through the snow, leaving impressions that might suggest large footsteps, but the tracks I had seen alternated in their orientation from left to right repeatedly, like a person's. Why would that happen if a coyote or other creature were leaping over the snow, assuming they could do that in the first place?

Sure enough, back down the trail, we came to the mysterious prints again. We noted that they went up through a rough terrain that seemed an unlikely path for a moose. It was hard to imagine a moose making that sixty-five-inch stride nearest the trail, agile as a moose can be, or placing its hind hooves so precisely where its front ones had landed, as might well be the case on more even ground. Indeed, the route seemed one more suitable to a creature on two legs, one that could place its feet judiciously, the way a very athletic person may negotiate such a landscape. Of course, an athletic person would have to be about eight feet tall to move so easily through such deep snow. Moreover, because there had been no thaw, there was little compacting of the lower levels of the snow cover such as might have diminished the depth to which a creature would sink, particularly a moose, which is the heaviest animal in the forest and one with hooves that would more likely sink farther than a human foot. One would expect a moose track to resemble that of a deer.

Later, at home, we searched through numerous pictures of tracks in snow. Many were surprisingly similar, but those that most resembled what I had found were on sites that posted supposed Sasquatch tracks. This, of course, did not constitute any proof of their identity. Our tracks had been snowed over and were partly filled in. We are left again with mystery. Certainly others have walked by those tracks and not for a moment assumed that they could be anything unusual, and maybe they're not.

March 31

Yesterday, we walked up the road and noticed tracks coming down through the forest with a shape that resembled that of the ones we had seen on the 7th. We didn't have time to investigate seriously but resolved to check them out the next day. When we did, it became clear that these were the impressions of snowshoes. Some did resemble a human foot, but others in the same line preserved the entire outline of the shoe, and all were close together. The tracks themselves had formed hard icy pedestals in the considerably melted snow. When a person or creature walks in the snow, the area under the foot is compacted, and with the melting and refreezing that occurs over time, this denser area hardens and often rises above the looser snow around it. I had found on a previous hike that I could walk more easily with normal boots if I stepped on snowshoe tracks, which had become like stepping stones. We decided to revisit what remained of the original prints to see if this pedestalling process might reveal anything. The length of that stride, over five feet in deep snow, still seemed to rule out a person on snowshoes.

It took us a while to find that old location, but I had photos on my phone that showed distinguishing landmarks, particularly two trees of different sizes growing very close together. We walked farther than I thought we would need to, and I might have turned back had Donna not insisted on continuing, but we did finally reach the two trees. We immediately saw the melted remnants of the tracks, our own and the creature's, as well as the wide impression where I had fallen as I attempted to wade through the deep snow. And indeed, after all the melting of the last few weeks, the compacted snow at the bottom of the tracks had partially risen above the surface, revealing a shape that looked very much like an extremely large human foot. Though partially melted, these reverse impressions were much bigger than my size-12 boots and, though lacking detail, suggested the outline of five toes. We knew they could not have been made by snowshoes since we had seen their former depth, even if someone had been improbably athletic enough to virtually leap over such deep snow.

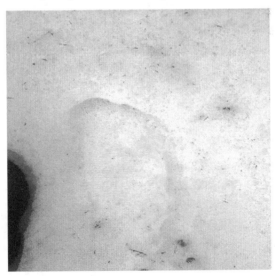

The tracks led up into the forest, disappearing in an open area of more sunlight, then resuming less distinctly over rocky terrain. Though quite deteriorated, certain of the prints did look like purported Sasquatch prints that have been cast over the years: more flat and wide with no suggestion of the distinctive arch of a human foot. For some reason – perhaps my personal fatigue with the whole subject that has been such a distraction – I was reluctant to think that these might indeed be Bigfoot tracks, but what other alternative could there be? Some gigantic person walking barefoot through the snow, someone with a five-foot-plus stride in three feet of snow who was so heavy that snowshoes failed to keep him from sinking?

When I look back on what has happened since September, I question my own judgement. Could I be attributing mundane phenomena to an imaginary being? Could Donna's eyes have been playing tricks on her? I suppose, but how would someone else in the same neighborhood have exactly the same experience? Did the strange noises we have heard come from known creatures, whose vocal repertoire is greater than most realize? I can't rule this out completely, but it's dubious. Could some accidental factors have left what looks like a hand print on the car? And then another? I don't see how, but doing so twice is really is beyond improbable. And now we have these tracks in the deep snow. I keep questioning myself but continue to conclude that the creature is real. Besides, there is another dimension to the whole subject, the weight of numerous similar stories coming from various times and places, not just reports of sightings, but other reported aspects of the experience of those who have had encounters.

People who claim to have encountered a Sasquatch seem almost universally to experience a kind of shock and fascination that can sometimes turn into obsession. I suspect that the creature embodies the deep archetype that Carl Jung referred to as the "wild man," a mythic image he encountered in various cultures. Never suspecting that such a real creature might exist, Jung recognized that the figure of the wild hairy man derived from deep mythology, from Enkidu in the ancient Sumerian epic of *Gilgamesh*, to Grendel, the hairy man-like monster of the Anglo Saxon epic *Beowulf*. We may suspect that the goblins of folklore and the orcs of Tolkien's *Lord of the Rings* represent at least the negative, frightful side of the archetype. There is no doubt that the image of the wild man is freighted with intense feelings, representing, it seems, our link to the animal kingdom, to instincts unmediated by civilization. Seeing a Sasquatch, or just encountering evidence of one like a footprint, can have a dramatic impact that is qualitatively different from the excitement one might feel at discovering some other rare or unknown species, even one like the bili apes, the giant chimpanzees recently found in the Congo.

It is understandable that the subject has given birth to numerous TV shows and documentaries. Perhaps the mythic resonance of the subject is in part responsible for its being largely ignored by academics. What serious biologist would go searching for a unicorn or sea serpent or any other creature long relegated to the realm of myth? Of course, it has commonly been the case that many real creatures were first thought to be mythical. When tales of the great apes in Africa first reached Europe, they were deemed untrue, perhaps because they reminded people of that wild man in folklore and myth. One might even question whether any of the creatures in myth do not have some basis in the natural world. Regardless, Sasquatch by many different names has existed for a long time in the human imagination.

May 2015

May 3

I have been out of Pelham since April 25. Donna is staying on for a while, perhaps till September. Recently, this whole series of experiences has receded into a kind of hazy unreality. It all seems so remote and almost irrelevant to our relationship issues and the need to get life practically on track. Down here on the outskirts of Northampton, even with all the forest and meadows of the river bottom close by, our Sasquatch seems the creature of a dream, an image that shone more brightly in the winter darkness and is now fading in the first bright sunny days of spring. Even a few reports from Jon Wilk about activity near the Pelham house, some newly discovered stick structures and two occasions on which researchers have had rocks thrown at them, somehow don't affect me all that much.

Last night, however, another event of note: When Donna got home and was heading for the front door, she heard two very loud whoops and a tree knock. That's what she just told me. There was nothing scary about it, she says; indeed, it was a reassuring and happy occurrence. She says the owls were out again and the whooping sound was completely different from their hoots. Again, the sounds came from the forest to the west. Could it have been some other creature? Of course, but she says she has found nothing similar except for supposed Sasquatch recordings and my own imitation of the call I heard last December.

May 11

This past Friday, the night after the noises described above, another suspicious event occurred. At about midnight, Donna reports, she heard the sound of rocks being struck sharply together, a clacking noise three times in quick succession, then again three times, then seven. She says it was very rhythmic, like quarter notes and quarter note rests spaced out over four measures of four, with rests on the final beat of the first two measures and of the fourth measure: 1 2 3 rest, 1 2 3 rest, 1 2 3 4,1 2 3 rest. The bedroom window was open and the noise came from down below in the yard. Chessi, the cat, came running into her room, immediately leapt up onto the desk by the window, and peered into the darkness, tail swishing back and forth. When Donna got up and looked out herself, she could see nothing. None of the outside lights was on, either at the neighbor's across the road or by the landlord's front door, which faces the same part of the yard.

Of course, we don't know what made the clacking sound outside the window. As usual, the signs are ambiguous. I do recall reading somewhere an account of Sasquatch knocking rocks together; I can't think where at the moment. But what could be doing so out in the dark yard in the middle of the night? Is there some other way of generating such a sound? And what of the cat's very unusual and curious reaction? The woods out there are full of creatures and noises. Coyote hybrids, foxes, owls, bears, fisher cats. Moose are common. No doubt all sorts of screams and growls can be accounted for by these known animals. But whoops and loud whistles, and now the clacking of rocks? We cannot help suspecting that our creature is trying to communicate with Donna. She, for her part, does not feel threatened but indeed continues to experience a kind of profound happiness whenever some new manifestation occurs. I can easily imagine our Sasquatch being somewhat entranced by her very beautiful golden hair, even when viewed from a considerable distance. Perhaps she is as wondrous a being to him as he is to her.

Last night, I reread Carleton Coon's brief essay, "Why There Has To Be a Sasquatch," found on the Bigfoot Encounters website. It's so interesting that such an eminent scientist reached the conclusion several decades ago that the creature is real, in part because of evidence from hair and blood samples, and that the evidence he refers to seems to have been lost or forgotten. What's that about? Also of note – Coon refers to early encounters in the east, not the northwest, and the case he investigated himself happened just over the New Hampshire border, in the same general area as our encounter. In the recent work by Jeff Meldrum I don't see any reference to Coon. Curious. Also, I don't believe that Melba Ketchum knows that there were early studies that seem to confirm her own conclusions based on genetic studies, that a real unknown hominin lives among us. Is this an example of selective forgetting? Does hard science, if at odds with conventional thinking or commercial interests, get swept under the rug? I guess the answer to that is obvious.

Reading this essay does take me back to my student days and that course in evolution I took at Harvard's Peabody Museum. William Howells was our professor. He was well known in the academic world of that time, and it was from Professor Howells that I first learned of Carleton Coon. Coon was a colorful figure, one who could have inspired a fictional character like Indiana Jones. Best known for his studies of the races of man, he held prominent posts at both Harvard and the University of Pennsylvania. He had a broader background than many scientists. He had studied Egyptian hieroglyphs and Greek at Phillips Academy Andover before entering Harvard as an undergraduate. In Cambridge, he studied Egyptology as well as Anthropology. He traveled to many remote places as an anthropologist and was even a spy in North Africa during World War 2, smuggling guns to French resistance groups in German-occupied Morocco. Coon was controversial and sometimes considered racist because he believed that different races and ethnic groups had evolved quite different capabilities, but he was also very much respected for the research he did. Not one to shy away from controversy, Coon boldly asserts the existence of Sasquatch in this essay and explains some of the evidence he personally has encountered:

Even before I read John Green's book Sasquatch: The Apes Among Us, *I accepted the Sasquatch's existence. A year ago, as representative of the Peabody Museum of Harvard, I was sent to a town in New Hampshire just over the Massachusetts border to investigate a sighting.*

A man who lived just below the border in Massachusetts had driven his pickup truck, which he had converted into a camper, to a wooded glade along a highway. He stopped there and went to sleep at the wheel, his two young sons likewise snoozing on bunks by a window.

At 11:00 p.m. the man awoke. Something was rocking his vehicle from side to side. An earthquake? He stepped out and was immediately grasped on the left shoulder by a seven-foot-tall creature covered with light brown or yellowish hair. Its right hand pushed the camper off his running board into the ground. It looked down on him and stuck out its tongue. The man jumped free, the creature stepped back. The man drove as fast as he could up the highway, the creature following him.

"Step on it, Dad!" the boys cried. "He's gaining on us!"

The creature apparently turned off the highway to the right, and then took another right into a so-called Lovers' Lane, where we later found physical evidence of perhaps what the lane had been named for.

I went there twice. The terrain was a deep mat of fallen white pine needles. Several weeks after the encounter, the prints of what had been going on were still depressed an inch and a half to two inches below the surface of the needles. Fully clothed, I weigh about 168 to 170 pounds, and wear size-12 shoes. My steppings and crawlings left no marks at all.

Coon goes on to describe other reports from the vicinity and notes similarities among witness accounts. He remarks on the state of shock in which he found the father and his two sons and points out that they passed polygraph tests. He goes on to report that a hair sample taken in Washington State from a barbed-wire fence leaves little doubt about the creature's existence. He also points out that there are numerous footprints that could not have been faked, including those he found on his investigation in New Hampshire.

Professor Stephen I. Rosen of the University of Maryland has identified its hair as that of a previously unknown primate--and he has hair on file for most of the living primates of the world. He has given me permission to state that its scale pattern is primate, its pigment dense and black like that of a lowland gorilla, and its internal structure "unusual." This last refers to the medulla of the hair strand, which is quite variable among the living races of man.

On this substantially impeccable evidence we may be justified to state that a primate other than man, which is either a pongid (ape) or hominin (kind of man), is alive in Washington, even if the hairs did not come off the animal identified as the creator of the local disturbance.

The blood that came with the hair has been examined by a professional in another institution. A newspaper report quotes him as saying that his sample is primate, possible human, but too degraded for further speculation.

Coon also reports that he made plaster casts of the footprints and impressions he found. Does this mean that in some specimen drawer in the bowels of the Peabody Museum there exist casts of Sasquatch tracks, tracks made in this very part of New England?

May 17

Nothing new to report in the way of encounters, but another series of interesting coincidences has occurred. Donna has been doing some genealogical research recently and has discovered that she is descended from certain Sherwoods, evidently a surname shared by many families in the neighborhood of Sherwood Forest. Naturally enough, she likes the associations with Robin Hood, Maid Marian, and a band of jolly outlaws in an old forest. However, there is more to the story. She decided to veg out with a look at "Finding Bigfoot," the TV show that we both find somewhat absurd given that no self-respecting Sasquatch is at all likely to be lured into range by a bunch of middle-aged guys crashing around in the woods with a camera crew, hooting and banging on trees. Evidently, in this episode, the team goes to Sherwood Forest where a Sasquatch "experiencer" believes he has been able to rouse a 'Squatch by clacking rocks together. Donna thought the whole episode silly. The witness never saw anything but was terrified by the sound of heavy feet, or more likely by his own imagination. Sasquatch in the UK? Probably only by way of television. Still, the clacking rocks in conjunction with Sherwood Forest and her genealogical work, all in the same week; well, it does seem weird. An odd coincidence.

May 21

Nothing could have been further from my mind than a Sasquatch in the woods of Western Massachusetts. I'd had a long day sorting out a minor renovation project, then played a traditional music session at The Harp with many of my friends and a pretty large audience. But later, shortly after I got home, Donna called me. Jon had left her a message. One of the researchers he knows saw today, near Gate 10, a *white* Sasquatch! Wilk, she said, was beside himself. It now appears that *three* people unbeknownst to each other have described the same being and all three encounters have happened within a few square miles. We don't know yet the details of this last sighting, but it is noteworthy that Gate 10 is very close to the Pelham house, closer than the earlier sightings. In fact, if those foot prints I found in March had continued through the forest in the general direction in which they were headed, they would have ended up near Gate 10. It is hard not to imagine a connection between this most recent sighting and the strange clacking together of rocks Donna heard last week outside in the yard around midnight.

Someone reading this might well suspect it all to be fiction. I, the narrator, am just a secondary character, bearing witness to the events, like Conrad's Marlowe, the man who was there, saw and heard much and learned the background histories of the principal characters, who would, in this case, be Donna and the Sasquatch. The story does have so many pop literary motifs. I imagine a comic book figure – Sasquatch, like so many superheroes, a kind of human hybrid, endowed with special powers, but of necessity a solitary being whose identity remains a secret from the outside world. Sasquatch, like other such characters, has one or a few humans with whom he is connected or even allied, but he is a lonely creature from a widely scattered and forgotten race who knows that secrecy is the key to his freedom and power. Though he is a giant, stronger than any other being in his domain, he can move rapidly with uncanny silence and disappear into the forest so quickly that he is believed by some to slip into another dimension. It is easy to get swept away by such phantasies, but I really know nothing about this creature's habits and social life.

I'm remembering something I've not mentioned before, that time last fall when Donna, from the top of Soapstone Hill, looked out over the reservoir and saw some white figure far away on the opposite shore. She turned to me to get my attention, but when we both looked to where she was pointing, neither of us could see anything. Was it some fisherman dressed in white, a trick of the eye, a birch tree catching the changing light and conjuring up a standing figure. I imagine a story unfolding. I see the Sasquatch standing briefly on the shore staring up to the hills beyond where he can see Donna perched on the highest rocky outcrop gazing down at the water. Perhaps for a second their eyes meet but at too great a distance for her to comprehend the connection though in that instant she sees him there and wonders. She looks at me and calls out, then focusing again on that far shore, sees nothing above the stony beach but the green of the forest. He has slipped away into the trees.

What will happen next? I expect we'll speak with Jon later today and get the full story. It would be interesting to meet the other witness. How many more might there be? Is the White Sasquatch a permanent resident of the accidental wilderness of the Quabbin? Are there others of his kind in the vicinity, perhaps a family group? Is Donna really having one of the more protracted encounters? Is the creature really trying to communicate with her and, if so, to what end? I stop myself, thinking this is all crazy, but the facts I've recorded say otherwise. I can only conclude that events of high strangeness and great significance are actually taking place.

May 23

Yesterday, we hiked from Gate 12. The map was misleading and we never reached the water, just descended into the forest till the path vanished under shrubs and new growth in what looked to be the remnants of a logging area. But during the walk, Donna noted an idea she had had about another strange occurrence, something she had not told me about before. At intervals of a month or more, small trinkets had appeared on the path outside the front door: a black onyx bead, a small gold four-leaf clover, a silver starfish, and a little angel made of some indeterminate metal. Several pieces of what appeared to be natural turquoise had also showed up on the ground. The objects were all bright enough to stand out against the dull gravel and dirt of the path, and their appearance had not been preceded by anyone's raking the area in such a way as to uncover something that might have been dropped at some point in the past. There they lay right on the surface. It's important to note that the little Pelham house has had very few visitors, just a handful of people other than Donna's daughters, neither of whom recognizes any of the tiny objects. Each of my own daughters has visited the house exactly once.

Donna showed me the trinkets last night. She had them safely stashed in a small bowl. It had never occurred to her before, but suddenly she could not help wondering if they had been tokens left by the creature. Of course, we both agreed this was a crazy idea, but somehow we could not dismiss it out of hand. Since our encounter in September and subsequent reading of other witnesses' experiences, we have found that some believe a Sasquatch will make such offerings, like the antique marbles described on the site Sasquatch Ontario. I always found this notion highly suspect, but some animals do in fact collect objects seemingly because they are attracted by a glittery appearance, crows and ravens for example. Both birds exist in this vicinity, but I've seen no nest nearby, and what are the chances of such objects being dropped repeatedly in the very same location? Once again, here we are spending time entertaining a silly notion, imagining a mythic – some would say monstrous – creature dropping baubles on the path, perhaps as tokens of affection, little gifts to Donna. We must be out of our minds. I really do want to hear what the newest witness of the White Sasquatch has to say. According to Jon's message, he is a retired police officer.

May 25

Something very odd happened Saturday night. I performed my song, *Old Stones, Broken Bones*, with Max Creek up at the Strange Creek festival in Greenfield, an annual outdoor event that always draws thousands of campers and music lovers. The band's original members are good friends, and they have done that song for years. There was nothing unusual about that; I've played that tune with them on many occasions. But back at Donna's, at just about the same time I stepped up to the microphone, that strange rhythmic tapping started up again in the back yard. I got her email when I returned to my place in Northampton.

She'd been sitting at the table in the living room, by the windows that look out into the yard. It was a very dark night and cold, so cold it had been uncomfortable for me as I waited to go on stage twenty miles north in Greenfield. Donna was sitting with her guitar, working on a song, when the sound started up. It was loud and clear and very close, she says, that same pattern she had heard before: 1 2 3 rest, 1 2 3 rest, 1 2 3 4, 1 2 3 rest. This time it was more metallic, like wood on metal. It could have been someone banging on the metal bulkhead leading to the basement, just yards from where she was sitting. She says she felt the sound was directed at her, a signal of some kind, and that she was being watched. She wondered if the landlord was up to something, but that made no sense. She jumped up and backed away from the window as Chessi hopped onto the table and peered out into the darkness, her tail swishing, just as she had when that clacking sound had started up on that other night. What was this sound that seemed to be directed at Donna? Was it a message? She had gone into the darkened kitchen and looked out into the yard through the back door window, but nothing was visible except the vaguely outlined shapes of the big pine trees at the edge of the lawn and the deeper black of the woods beyond. Then, as she was about to fearfully gather her things and head upstairs, she suddenly felt calm, somehow knew that everything was alright. She sat back down right by the window. Her son called, and while he was on the phone, she even pressed her face against the glass but again could see nothing unusual.

May 30

I am back in Pelham for the weekend. We stayed up very late, talking about our relationship and all the issues we have been dealing with over the past year and, of course, discussing the creature and speculating about those improbable rhythms in the darkness. It is so odd that Donna felt, this last time, assured enough somehow to return to her seat near the window rather than retreating to her bedroom on the second floor. We have joked about how, when we are sitting in the living room, it is as if we are in a fishbowl, 'Squatches outside watching if they want to be.

This morning as we talked about our first encounter on September 22, we recalled vividly certain aspects of the experience that I may not have noted in as much detail as I should have. Why on such a beautiful evening had I been so oddly concerned about getting back to the car before the light faded? It was a relatively short walk. Even as we sat by the water, had I unconsciously sensed the unnatural quiet, the absence of bird songs and the typical insect noises? I do remember worrying about being out as darkness fell even though the trail was a wide old road, the sky clear, and the distance to the car not that far.

Then there was Donna's reaction. I remember the expression on her face when I turned back to see her staring off into the woods – puzzled but almost beatific, smiling so broadly. As she described what she had seen, I became increasingly alarmed. Why? I was absolutely certain that what she had seen was a real Sasquatch, even though nothing could have been more unexpected. I should have been incredulous when she described a head and long arms, but instead, my reaction was immediate and the opposite of hers. It was as if I, myself, had just seen as clear as day some dangerous animal, a grizzly bear for example. She, on the other hand, felt a sense of wonder and peace and wanted to linger on the path, while I began moving at a pace just short of a panicked run. And I had seen nothing at all!

And then there was the color of the creature, the bright white of its hair, almost luminous to a degree seemingly impossible for a being living in the forest.

Donna does not struggle for an explanation of these strange events. She seems to find refuge in the mystery of it all, even as she faces her inevitable departure from this place in the fall. She imagines a woman who lived here back in 1790 and wonders what her thoughts were as she looked out these same windows. What were her fears, her hopes? Donna once relied on a church community for some kind of spiritual fellowship. She was even a missionary who traveled with a group to Yugoslavia. How different that is from anything I might have done, attempting to spread a religious message born in the matrix of evangelical America back to the old world. Any woman living here in 1790 would have almost certainly been a church-going Christian and would have no doubt seen more intimately the frailty of the human condition. There would have been signs and wonders enough in old Bible stories. The natural world was a place to be conquered and put to use, a creation arranged by the creator, with all its perils and hardship, still a place where the notion of some half-human creature would have probably been unthinkable, unless as a terrifying, demonic disruption of the divine order. Yet here was Donna sensing a strong kinship with that unnamed woman as well as with our mysterious visitor. She had left the church long before I met her, but somehow this whole experience seemed to have a spiritual dimension, as if the very otherness of it all offered some kind of haven. Odd, considering the frightening aspects of the Sasquatch, if that is really what we are dealing with.

May 31

Yesterday, we went back to Gate 26, the location of some of the beautiful vistas we've photographed. The old road that leads down to the water is open for a good distance so you can drive much of

the way and only walk the last mile or so. Just as we were nearing
the closed gate, we noticed that a small tree was bent down across
the road so that its top, still full of new green foliage, lay on the
dirt. We stopped so that I could pull the tree aside by grabbing the
narrow upper part of the trunk. When Donna drove past and I
released the tree, it sprang back across the road. As I examined it,
I could see that the trunk had broken and split about six feet above
the ground. It had been bent over, then pulled further down by some
tremendous weight or force exerted far enough up the trunk to pull
the woody fibers apart where the tree was still about five inches
thick. I climbed up the bank of the roadway to examine it more
closely. There were no cut marks, or signs of any impact, just that
section where enough force had been applied to literally tear the
trunk apart. There was no remnant of another nearby tree that might
have fallen down and bent it over with sufficient force to leave it
down across the road. The ground around the trunk was hard, no
doubt due to the lack of rain, and covered with compacted flattened
leaves that had lain under winter snow till about two months ago.
The leaves on the bank were more disturbed, most of them
obviously from my own scrambling up the incline. The tree was
about twenty-five feet tall, a young beech. There was nothing to
suggest a lightning strike, no indication of some microburst or
extreme weather capable of twisting trees. The surrounding forest
was undisturbed. Something had pulled the tree down. Of course,
we both had our suspicions. The tree did seem like a "Do Not
Enter" sign, an attempt to discourage intrusions. Donna was
uneasy, but for some reason, I felt unconcerned. I guess we had
switched roles. We parked just down the road at the DCR gate and
walked to the water.

The day was beautiful. We hiked along the shore, lingering in one of the back coves for a while, observing a large bass cruising in the shallows. We even spotted a loon on one of the islands, sitting on her nest, and were able to photograph her with my simple optical zoom. We headed back about 7, knowing that we still had plenty of daylight left to reach the car. About fifteen minutes into the trail, we were startled by the sound of a tree crashing in the forest slightly behind us and off to our right. Donna was alarmed. I still felt little concern. Old trees regularly drop whole sections. Heavy branches that may have been rotting for twenty years suddenly fall in a slight gust of wind, I reassured her, but she definitely had a sense that the sound had been some kind of warning.

Later that evening, we found various reports of Sasquatches breaking or pulling down trees in displays intended as warnings, or primitive "No Trespassing" signs. We even saw some quite remarkable video footage from Ohio (the Brown video) that did seem to illustrate this behavior. Again, the coincidences seem to be accumulating with improbable frequency. Donna confided in me that she had been scared. A voice inside her head had told her, "You're not out of the woods yet." She had thought that funny; then the voice had added, "I'm not kidding." She was worried. Was she betraying "their" trust, being too curious, becoming an intruder? She had heard another phrase in her mind that seemed a kind of explanation: "It's about the researchers." I suppose a creature whose security and freedom depends on secrecy could be threatened by a spreading awareness of its existence.

Given the recent patterned sounds and now the broken and crashing trees, I do suspect we are once again experiencing typical behaviors of the creature, not just the random effects of weather or the growth and decay of trees in the forest. Am I crazy to think such thoughts? One other point: Our plans for the day had nothing to do with Sasquatch research. We really wanted to visit one of the more beautiful shorelines, looking for driftwood and birdlife and enjoying the scenery. We did not expect to have any encounters and never saw this area as a likely place for Sasquatch research.

June 2015

June 1

It was interesting to read in the BFRO section on behavior this morning the following passages:

Their strength, especially upper body, is legendary. They seem to take "pleasure" in exercising this strength, for example, lifting basketball-sized rocks and throwing them in arcs to scare off intruders, lifting the edges of mobile homes, cars or trailers, lifting and throwing full 50 gal. drums (450 lbs.) or 240 lb rocks (weighed later), and spirally twisting the trunks of small trees, possibly as territorial or way markers.

Vocalization and Communication

On the whole, the Sasquatch proceeds in silence. Patterned, repetitive knocking sounds, produced with rocks or thick branches hit against other rocks or dead trees, are apparently used as long-distance communication or deterrence.

Today we went back to the place of the broken tree. It was still as I had left it. Donna was again uneasy and rain began to fall steadily. I took a couple of pictures through the open car window but saw no reason to get out. On the road down here, I had noticed how many tall saplings were bent over, forming little archways among the dominant forest trees. They had grown fast, I thought, competing for the light, but not developing enough thickness or lateral strength to hold up against the ice and snow. Some had died, but none were broken like the tree that blocked the road. Moreover, the top part of the broken tree was more or less straight and stretched down to the road at a defined angle. It was bent most noticeably closer to the spot where the wood had given way, splitting apart vertically and tearing from whatever force had been applied above it. It occurs to me now that the force must therefore have been applied at about eleven or twelve feet above the ground. I consider that this height is just about where a tall Sasquatch would naturally grasp a tree it wanted to pull over. Could a very large bear have exerted this much force? I don't see why one would have climbed such a narrow tree, located amidst other trees, and I cannot imagine a bear being heavy enough or gaining enough leverage to tear the wood apart. Was there some flaw in the wood, some disease in the heart of the tree? Even if there were, it seems unlikely that this could have created such weakness that any normal creature could break it.

We didn't stay more than a few minutes. Donna did not want to linger there, facing downhill at the end of a blocked-off dirt road. We backed up into a flat open area to turn around and headed up out of the forested valley. I know I glanced nervously in the rear-view mirror. We went off for a Sunday drive, browsing around an old antique store in Northfield where the prices for even the most useless junk were exorbitant, checking out the lake at Erving State Forest, and ending up unintentionally on the road to her father's old house. We briefly visited his grave at the nearby cemetery. Donna missed him very much. He had been a great outdoorsman, the person who most instilled in her a love of nature, who had often taken her hiking and camping. Again, as we drove through this countryside of many memories, we wondered what in the world had happened to our lives, how nothing had turned out as expected, and how we could possibly have found ourselves so preoccupied with such an overwhelmingly strange subject as the White Sasquatch. We were no longer living together though we spent a great deal of time in each other's company. Donna had not really started up her business, and I had not written any more of that family history project in several months.

June 4

Yesterday, I went up to Donna's after working in Amherst and doing a few errands. She told me of a very odd coincidence. She had been talking to a close friend, an extremely brilliant young woman who had taken an interest in the apparent significance of certain sets of numbers. I've read about such ideas. An example that comes to mind is the Finbonacci Series or Golden Mean, which seems to be displayed in nature and is sometimes considered an important ratio in aesthetics as well. I have never progressed much beyond understanding pi and have always been mystified by the more abstract reaches of mathematics. Both Donna and her friend are way beyond me in this regard. I have noticed odd coincidences clustered around certain numbers, but whatever meaning they've had for me I attribute to some kind of synchronicity, to use the Jungian term, not an inherent quality of the numbers themselves. Donna's friend had recently noticed that the number series 3,3,7 seemed to be occurring with meaningful frequency in her own life, the *very same sequence that was drummed out by the clacking together of rocks and the rapping Donna heard outside her window on the Saturday night of Memorial Day weekend!* What, if anything, are we to make of this? Are we to imagine a Sasquatch tapping out messages in a kind of mathematical code?

As we were talking later in the day, planning out an evening walk, we dismissed going back to the area of the tree that had been pulled down. We had speculated about going there and cutting out the section of the break, five or six feet of the trunk that we or anyone else could examine in an attempt to explain how it could have broken as it did. We didn't go back there mainly because Donna was not feeling all that well and it was a bit far to drive.

Last night, when I woke up sometime in the wee hours and got up briefly, I found myself thinking about our idea of retrieving that section of the broken tree. Suddenly, I became alarmed at the idea. Did I want to be the guy responsible for taking down a Sasquatch's

"No Trespassing" sign? If we were going to get that piece of wood, I would prefer letting some ranger clear the obstructing section of the tree off the road first. Then, there were the words that had come to Donna's mind: "It's about the researchers." All of this is crazy. But hadn't a white Sasquatch just shown himself to a researcher, that retired policeman? I went to sleep thinking of these conflicting ideas.

June 8

This afternoon, I went up to Pelham to visit Donna and check out a new discovery she made over the weekend. Near a parking area at a place called Hank's Meadow, she'd noticed a strange teepee-like stick structure, similar to the one she'd found in the woods behind her home. She'd spotted it while hiking up to the big stone tower overlooking the reservoir when her siblings were with her during their reunion get-together. They didn't stop to examine it, and only she considered the possibility that it might have been anything other than a project by some kids. I almost said "campers" but there are no campers allowed anywhere in the watershed and there are rangers who make sure visitors are out by dusk. They routinely check all the roads for unattended vehicles or other signs of stragglers. Hank's Meadow is a long field that sweeps down to the water. It is bordered by a young, mixed-hardwood forest in which a few very old trees are scattered, trees that must have once provided shade for cattle on the sloping pastures of the Swift River Valley. The curious teepee structure was just twenty or thirty yards into the forest next to the parking area at the top of the meadow. A circle of long poles and small tree trunks had been placed upright around a cluster of four tall young maples, all of which appeared to share the same root system. If one had wrapped hides about the framework, it would have very much resembled the classic dwelling of the plains Indians.

At first glance, I assumed this was some childish project, but as I walked closer, the whole construction appeared more and more bizarre. First of all, the area, in summer at least when it is accessible, is very visible. The structure was about twenty feet tall and had required moving some big pieces of wood, not the kind of activity allowed in the park. Moreover, several of the pieces were very heavy, the largest among them a twenty-foot leader from an ancient maple that stood a short ways off in the forest. This double-trunked tree was very wide and tall with several thick dead branches rising up fifty or sixty feet above the ground. These branches looked like the biggest piece of the teepee – dead but very hard, weathered wood, the kind that makes hot, long-lasting fires. At first, I wondered if this largest upright log had simply grown where it was standing, then fallen over into its present position. No, it was not attached to any stump, just placed there on the ground and leaned up there. But how? And by whom? It must have weighed hundreds of pounds. And how would one lift it high enough to make it vertical and topple it over? Even several strong men would have been hard pressed to lift such a weight. How could they have lifted it high enough to rest so far up against the supporting maples? Ropes and pulleys? If I were strong enough to lift this big tree limb and hold it over my head with its base on the ground, I couldn't have achieved nearly the angle required. If I had blocked the base and pushed it up till it toppled over, well then I would have been one strong fellow indeed, stronger than any other human, and it would have been extremely hard to control the direction of its fall. This was clearly not some Boy Scout engineering project. Moreover, the top of this largest element in the structure had to be placed quite precisely to fit in the narrow gap between the tree trunks. We checked the surrounding trees, but there was clearly no neighbor from which this branch could have dropped accidentally. It had to have been dragged or carried, then raised somehow into position. I am familiar with the art of moving heavy objects with simple levers. As a young man, I sometimes helped my father set up equipment for the well-drilling jobs he did. Without any regular helper, he frequently moved very heavy steel bits for his drilling machine, and I learned many of his tricks. I once made a decent paycheck by taking down an old barn by myself in order to salvage its chestnut beams. If I and a couple of strong helpers had wanted to build this teepee structure, we would have needed, at the very least, a straight forked pole to significantly extend the height to which we could have pushed up the heavy tree limb, much the way sheet rockers use cross tees to put up ceilings.

So once again, we are confronted with a mystery. I'm not saying this has to be the handiwork of our friend. The whole discussion of tree structures has always seemed dubious to me. So many would-be Sasquatch researchers are running around attributing significance to every time two tree branches fall in such a way as to make an X. But I will note that the strange teepee is only a short walk from where that other witness we found online reported seeing a white 'Squatch. Here is another enigmatic phenomenon. The structure is crude and seemingly of no practical value. If people built it, they must have done so in daylight when the ground was free of snow, and they would have been very conspicuously violating watershed regulations, which very clearly define permissible activities – hiking, fishing with a valid license in season in certain areas, and biking on designated trails or roads. And yet, if this were one of the purported Sasquatch "tree structures," why on Earth would it have been placed near such a well-traveled area?

Could it be an attempt at communication? Am I missing something obvious? Are there people somewhere who could explain how and why they built it? Do any of the rangers know about this? Have they just assumed without looking closely that some day trippers built the structure? Maybe we can answer those questions. Certainly our creature could have done this kind of work at night, given his nocturnal habits. So here I am again, speculating in a way that I am sure is likely to provoke laughter among the "unbelievers." While I'm offering myself up as a sacrifice to the gods of ridicule, I should also note one more coincidence from the last few days. Donna tells me that two nights ago, "Finding Bigfoot" investigated a tree that had been pulled down and broken just like that one we found last week. Cliff Barackman, Donna says, expressed skepticism about many of the tree structures and breaks people attribute to Sasquatch. However, in some cases, like that of our broken tree or the structure in Hank's Meadow, he is hard pressed for another explanation.

June 16

Yesterday, we took the day off to celebrate Donna's birthday. We drove up to Winchendon where she wanted to visit a store run by Native Americans, which sells native arts and related goods. The woman managing the place for the day, Sandy, was friendly and talkative. Donna, to my surprise, asked her if she knew anything about how native cultures viewed tales of Sasquatch. She has been extremely reluctant to talk about the subject with anyone but me for reasons that I still don't fully understand. However, in this setting she was perfectly comfortable to broach the subject. Sandy said that among her own ancestors, the Seminoles, there was a belief that the creature could shapeshift into other beings, a black panther for example. All native cultures, she thought, believed the creature was real. In eastern Canada and Maine, where she has attended the most native gatherings, there was a strong belief in the existence of the being, although reactions to it seemed to include both a sense of joy and wonder and one of fear. I was reminded of my own reaction and Donna's on that September hike when the creature appeared.

June 22

We spoke to Jon Wilk on Saturday. He was anxious to see the stick structure we had found and noted that he had seen about thirty over the years, many involving larger logs that humans could not have lifted. He said that he had recently started working with the Bigfoot Researchers Organization, the BFRO, and had more witness reports than he could investigate, clustered, it seems, in our area and out closer to Boston near the Great Swamp. He seemed a little unnerved and expressed frustration. "None of this makes sense," he said. He seemed to be wondering why in the world he had spent so much time trying to understand and communicate with the elusive forest giants. How could their presence be so obvious from time to time even as they remained invisible? The other night, he had heard a loud thump on the wall of his house but seen nothing when he looked out the window.

Last night, Donna had trouble sleeping. At one point I heard her get out of bed and walk over to the window. "Are you awake?" she asked. We started talking. "Look how dark it is," she said, "like that night when I heard the rocks clacked together." I got up and joined her at the window. Indeed, it was so dark outside, even with all the inside lights turned off, that we could distinguish none of the features of the yard below. A person standing right beneath the window would have been invisible to us. We talked for a while, Donna, like Jon the day before, questioning herself about what she was doing, wondering why on Earth the plans she had made the previous year no longer held her interest. Here she was, the straight-A grad student, a member of Mensa, spending every possible moment hiking in the forest and at night, when she might have been developing a business plan, reading about other people's encounters with Bigfoot and writing about her own experience.

Maybe we'll get together with Jon later today. In the meantime, he promised to give Matt, the other witness of the White Sasquatch, our contact info. He thought this man would want to connect with us.

Donna definitely feels connected to the White Sasquatch. That trail where she saw him, the easy walk to the calming waters of the Quabbin, had been a refuge for her in years past. She only remembered one other time when she had encountered another person, though she had sometimes walked there with her daughter. The path had seemed a place of safety, especially during some difficult times. Now she wonders if the white one was there watching, even back then. Perhaps he has known her for a long time, she speculates. I should find this idea crazy, but of course, I don't.

That feeling of being watched, it's common enough, and Rupert Sheldrake, the British biologist, has even written a book about it: *The Sense of Being Stared At*. He postulates a kind of directed energy field that accounts for it. Donna tells me that years ago when she lived in Seattle, Washington, near Mt. Rainier, she often felt an invisible presence watching her. She describes how the mountain in all its vastness would remain hidden for weeks, lost among clouds in the sky. Then, when the weather would finally clear, it would rise up out of the mist like some forgotten kingdom, dominating the landscape. One very sunny day, she drove to the mountain and ascended as far as the road and weather would permit. As she climbed, conditions worsened, snow showers turned to blinding squalls, and she could go no farther. Above her and below her were nothing but sky and mountain, an immensity lost in the swirling whiteout. She felt that someone was there, watching; she wonders if that experience has anything to do with the feeling she has had since our encounter. Is the awe inspired by a mountain or a mysterious, powerful being somehow connected to that feeling of being watched, perhaps the way religious people feel that they are always "seen" by God?

Donna's memory of driving up Mt. Rainier coincided eerily with my discovery of a very strange story from the nineteenth century. I found it on the website Bigfoot Encounters, but have since seen it elsewhere, including in a respected book on mountaineering: *The Challenge of Rainier*, by Dee Molenaar

E.S. Ingraham was a highly educator, the first superintendent of schools for the city of Seattle. In 1875, Ingraham immigrated to Seattle from Maine where he had attended Eastern Maine State Normal School and begun a career in teaching. He had also pursued classical studies at the Waterville Classical Institute. He seems to have been an exemplary Victorian intellectual; he oversaw the development of Seattle's public school system as its population grew from two hundred students to seventeen hundred. It's easy to forget how small a town Seattle was not that long ago and how wild were its surroundings. The nearby wilderness fascinated Ingraham, and he became a well-known mountaineer, best remembered today for his explorations of Mt. Rainier. Ingraham Glacier is named after him.

He recorded a bizarre encounter that happened during his exploration of caves in the crater of the mountain. This story is so strange that it is hard to imagine any respectable Victorian making it up or even imagining such a thing. Ingraham recounts his meeting with a creature he calls "the old man of the crater," a being he describes in terms that suggest he is talking about a Sasquatch. We have no way of knowing whether Ingraham had ever heard any tales about Bigfoot, but most people of his time had not. What is weirdest about this story is this being's paranormal ability to transfer its thoughts telepathically and the strange electrical phenomena Ingraham sees in the cave and in the creature itself. This is the stuff of science fiction, not your typical nineteenth-century explorer's narrative. What on Earth is going on here? Is this another confirmation of the sense that there is a strong psychic field (whatever that is!) connected to the creature? Discovering this piece somehow seems an important moment in our story. At least it has been for me. I can't say exactly why but I'm including this in my journal along with an excerpt from the original account.

In the following scene, Ingraham returns to a cave he had explored earlier in the day. He had seen bizarre scuff marks and "depressions that might have been made by some flat-footed animal." He had also noticed an odd glow in the atmosphere of the cave and felt in his body some kind of electrical current. It is particularly strange that Ingraham chooses to return to the cave alone, at night while his companions are sleeping. Why on Earth would he do this? For dramatic effect? Was he dreaming? If he were trying his hand at fiction, why didn't he say so rather than include this among his factual mountaineering accounts? Does some unknown force draw him back to the cave?

I had reached a point where another passage joined, or more properly separated from the one I was following, when I was startled by a noise, followed by several stones rolling down the tributary passage. Had my companion of the first visit noticed the mysterious things I had, and was he, like myself, seeking to discover their cause? I quickly stepped within a recess in the wall of ice on my left and awaited developments.

I had not long to wait, for almost immediately there came, now rolling, now making an attempt to crawl, a figure of strange and grotesque appearance, down the passage. It stopped within a few feet of me, writhing and floundering very much as a drowning man would do, when, drawn from the water, he was about to sink for the last time. Its shape was nearer that of a human being than of any other animal. The crown of its head was pointed, with bristled hair pointing in every direction. The eyeballs were pointed, too; and while they appeared dull and visionless at times, yet, there was an occasional flash of light from the points, which increased in frequency and brilliancy as the owner began to revive. The nails of

*its fingers and toes were long and pointed and resembled polished
steel more than hardened cuticle.*

*I discovered that the palms of its hands and the soles of its feet
were hard and calloused. In fact, the whole body, while human in
shape, except for the pointedness of the parts I have mentioned,
seemed very different in character from that of the human species.
There was nothing about the mysterious being, however, that would
make it impossible that its ancestry of long ages ago might have
been human beings like ourselves. Yet by living in different
surroundings and under entirely different conditions, many of its
characteristics had changed.*

*By degrees this strange being began to revive. Gradually an
electric glow covered the entire body with light-centers at the ends
of those pointed nails, the eyes, and the top of the head. It seemed
to accomplish its revivification by rubbing its hands vigorously
together. As soon as it was able to stand, it began to rub its feet
rapidly upon the floor of the cave. This increased the glow of its
body and caused the light-centers to shine with increased
brilliancy. It seemed to receive some vital fluid from the earth that
at once gave new vigor to its whole system. Involuntarily I imitated
its actions and immediately found myself undergoing a very
peculiar sensation. I seemed to be growing in accord with the
strange being who then for the first time noticed my presence. He
at once redoubled his former movements. He would rub his hands
vigorously together and then quickly extend the points of his fingers
in my direction when sparks of light would dart therefrom.*

*Having become deeply interested in this strange exhibition, I
went through the same maneuver with a similar result although
apparently in a much lesser degree. The effect was magical! I was
becoming* en rapport *with the Old Man of the Crater! I could see a
brilliant point of light gradually forming on the crown of his head.
Feeling my own hair beginning to rise, I removed my knit cap and
felt my hair bristling upward to a common point. The light from his*

crown seemed to form an arch above and between us and WE WERE IN COMMUNICATION. There, in that icy passage connecting the unknown interior of this earth with the exterior, by means of a new medium, or rather an old medium newly applied, two intelligent beings of different races were enabled to communicate, imperfectly at first of course, with each other.

For an hour I received impressions from the Old Man of the Crater. It is a strange story I got from him. While the time was comparatively short, yet what he told me, not by voice or look, but by a subtle agency not known or understood by me, would fill a volume of many pages. Finally expressing doubt at what he communicated, he commanded me to follow him. I had anticipated such a demand and was ready to resist it. So when he turned to descend, to the hot interior of the earth as I verily believe, by a superhuman effort I broke the spell and hastened upward and back to my sleeping companions.

This is no myth. The old man told me of his abode in the interior, of another race to which he belonged and the traditions of that race, of convulsions and changes on the earth long, long ago, of the gradual contraction of a belt of matter around the earth until it touched the surface hemming in many of the inhabitants and drowning the remainder, and of the survival of a single pair. All was shut out and the atmosphere became changed. Gradually this remaining pair was enabled to conform to the new order of things and became the parents of a race which for want of a better name I will call Sub-Rainians. This old man of the Crater had wandered far away from the abode of his race in his desire to explore. Far away from my home we had met, each out of his usual sphere.

"Each out of his usual sphere"; that phrase seems to describe the feeling I've had since Donna saw the White Sasquatch, a sense that in this eighteenth-century cottage and the nearby forests, different realities were converging.

Shortly after I wrote my last entry, I absent-mindedly picked up the book, *Psychic Sasquatch*, by Kewaunee Lepsaratis, which was lying on the nightstand in the bedroom, a work I had presumed to be a largely delusional account of imaginary connections among Bigfoot, UFOs, and God knows what other denizens of the human imagination. I, like Jon and Donna, was beginning to wonder about the weird coincidences that seemed to accompany each new manifestation of our "Sasquatch Experience." How much of our evolving story was an illustration of some bizarre psychological syndrome? Could all of this be dismissed with some new classification in the Diagnostic and Statistical Manual of Mental Disorders: "Contact with Mythical Beings Disorder" or some such malady that might be cured with the latest FDA approved pharmaceutical? What the hell was I doing? I flipped open the book, expecting some nonsense about Bigfoot as bearer of interplanetary wisdom from our space brothers in the constellation Orion. What did I see but the letterhead of Dr. Barry Fell of the Epigraphic Society in San Diego, California. Beneath was a letter regarding the translation of a certain inscription written in the Pre-Roman Iberian script that, as I already knew, Dr. Fell had studied extensively!

Many years before, Barry Fell had made headlines in my home town of Katonah, New York. The article had been captioned something like "Harvard Professor Cites Evidence of Early Celtic Seafarers in Local Stone Works." Fell was a marine biologist at Harvard but an amateur linguist in his spare time, an old-school scholar with a background in Greek and Latin and a passion for deciphering the early forms of writing that had proliferated before the Roman Empire. He had discovered in New England inscriptions on stone that he identified as Ogham, a primitive alphabet used by Celtic peoples, and thus had inferred, logically enough, that these early navigators had made it to North America. He also suggested that some of the enigmatic stone chambers in

New England and New York were probably the work of these people, since identical building techniques had been used in Europe. One such chamber had been a favorite haunt for me and some of my friends as teenagers, so I found the story particularly fascinating. I had read Fell's books and became interested in the early Celts and other peoples whose monuments like Stonehenge and Avebury remain largely mysterious. I even wrote a song that became somewhat well known in certain circles, "Old Stones, Broken Bones," which was inspired by my fascination with Fell's work. It was this song I was performing with the band Max Creek on the night when Donna had heard for the second time the mysterious pattern 3,3,7 tapped out close to the window where she was sitting. Before either she or I had any idea that we would encounter a mysterious creature, one of our mutual interests was the stone chambers in our immediate area. Indeed, one such chamber was embedded in a hillside a short walk from the house. Certainly Barry Fell never expressed an interest in the subject of Sasquatch. He was a biologist specializing in echinoderms, a kind of sea worm. His linguistic studies had nothing to do with strange notions about mysterious creatures and were only connected to his academic position tangentially. In his research travels across the oceans of the world, he had noticed certain rock inscriptions that demonstrated how far some early seafarers had sailed and whetted his appetite for solving the mysteries encoded in forgotten scripts. Epigraphy, the study of writing, was a science like marine biology, a web of evolving connections demonstrated by changes in written language, much as evolution is demonstrated by the different classes of species.

What the devil was a letter from Barry Fell doing in a book called *Psychic Sasquatch*? I read through the preceding page. The author, Kewaunee Lapseritis, was recounting the experience of a woman who purportedly had a relationship with a group of Sasquatch. They were actually friends. When one of them knelt down to closely examine her infant grandchild and she expressed concern for the safety of the baby, the Squatch was evidently offended and scratched four characters in the dirt. She had copied these characters, and sometime later, Lapseritis had sent them without explanation to Fell at the Epigraphic Society and asked if he could identify them. Fell, assuming he was looking at some rock inscription, confidently explained that the four characters were Iberian Punic and could be read as meaning "protected place." He wanted photographs and more information about the location so he could include the discovery in the forum section of the *Journal of Epigraphy.*

I have no idea what to make of this, but in keeping with my intention to simply report events as they unfold, I feel compelled to write it down. Dr. Fell has passed away. I'd like to see a physical copy of the letter he wrote. Assuming he did write the letter, a question arises in my mind: Did any of his books or publications include such an inscription that Lapseritis could then have used to construct a hoax, by sending Fell an inscription that his own writing had revealed? Because such early writing was quite crude and somewhat formulaic, the words might not have aroused the suspicion in Fell that he himself was the source of the inscription. It might have seemed the equivalent of finding an ancient inscription that read "No Trespassing," a phrase one would expect to find repeatedly in certain contexts. Universities aren't chock full of eager PhDs disputing the significance of the most recently discovered Punic inscription, and Lapseritis might well have known of Fell's work, particularly since he used to live in Western Massachusetts where Fell did some research. Were it not for the personal significance of Fell's books and Donna's and my mutual interest in the local stone chambers, an interest that has been eclipsed by the White Sasquatch, I would not have even bothered to think about something as whacked out as the notion that a Bigfoot could communicate reassurances to a worried grandmother by scratching out one of the most obscure forms of ancient writing in the dirt of an Oregon campground.

I'll mention two other incidents from the last couple of weeks that Donna reported to me. Who knows if they are in any way related, but they are strange. One night, she heard the sound of someone moving the latch on the front door. It is made of black iron, old fashioned looking in keeping with the rest of the little 1790 cottage. You press down a lever with your thumb and the latch lifts, clicking distinctively as it strikes the top of the mechanism. A modern deadbolt above is what actually locks the door. Donna was not all that concerned about this. She admitted that something else might have made the sound, though I am not sure she believed it. What was stranger was a noise that happened just a few nights earlier, but also when I was not around. She heard a loud crash that seemed to come from downstairs, after which the house was completely quiet as usual. When she turned on the hall light, everything looked normal. She thought perhaps the cat Chessi had knocked something over, unlikely unless she was chasing some mouse, since she is such a sure-footed little being. The noise seemed to come from the bottom of the stairs, near the door, but nothing looked amiss. She did not venture downstairs, but in the morning she found that nothing in any other part of the house had been knocked over. When she looked outside the front door, everything there was also in order.

June 26

The last two days have brought some significant developments. I was back in Pelham Wednesday night. After a walk of several miles through the Cadwell Forest, we put together a great dinner, then did a really productive run-through of some of the music we play together. During a late afternoon hike, Donna had noticed some odd configurations of fallen wood, a very obvious and symmetrical X and one slender sapling that was suspended between two trees so that it formed the lower half of a circle. None of this particularly impressed me. In a vast forest with many thousands of deadfalls occurring in any given year, some will always by chance look like they were placed there intentionally. There are real enough stick structures that someone obviously created, and Donna and I are both aware that obsessing about every possible sign of a visit by our hairy friend is not healthy or instructive. Our evening was pleasantly devoid of ponderings about our ongoing encounter, some of which we realized could well be an imaginative interpretation of ordinary events.

I woke briefly just before dawn to a metallic tapping sound coming through the open window. As I became conscious of my surroundings, the sound stopped and my first thought was, "Who could be working on some handyman project outside in the dark at four in the morning?" Then, the tapping started again, repeated rhythmically *seven* times, and stopped. I immediately thought of the rhythmic pattern Donna had told me she'd heard. Could I have heard the final sequence in the pattern? Was the sound really that of objects striking together? Sometimes a blue jay makes a mechanical-sounding call. Was I misinterpreting what I had heard? It was silent outside and still dark. As I lay there wondering, I did hear the first tentative birdsong, the brief fluid chirp of a robin. I still only saw darkness outside and soon fell back into a heavy sleep.

In the morning, I rose early, went downstairs, and worked at the computer. Donna did not come down till about ten. "How did you sleep?" I asked.

"Not well. Just at dawn a noise in the yard woke me, a kind of huffing or grunting outside. I almost got up to look outside but stayed in bed. I eventually did get up because I could not fall back to sleep. It was starting to get light, but I saw nothing unusual outside. I didn't get back to sleep till 7."

We thought about the noise she had heard. Maybe it was a bear. We've never seen one in the area, but they are common. Whatever it was, the sound must have come from a large animal.

As we sat together over coffee, we both felt some concern over the amount of time we had devoted to trying to understand the bizarre experiences that had been accumulating since Donna's sighting of the White Sasquatch. Even if we turned our account into a book, what would be the outcome of such an effort? We both had other completely unrelated career concerns that needed our attention. Whatever money might be generated, we would be exposing ourselves to potential ridicule or worse, accusations that we had fabricated a story for financial gain. Not that books in the current cultural climate are exactly the path to riches. We didn't discuss those consequences explicitly, but they were certainly on my mind, even though I had been much less reluctant to talk about the experience than Donna.

Now that the story seemed to be demanding that I record increasingly implausible happenings, I myself was feeling uncertain. I had imagined that we were encountering an amazing creature, probably a close relative of man, a sort of super-primate intelligent enough to avoid humans while living in the modern world. This was an astonishing proposition, but not inherently at odds with a modern scientific viewpoint. Indeed, the best scientists, primatologists, and specialists who could look at the evidence with a detailed understanding of anatomy and natural history seemed the least skeptical. Donna was clearly feeling stressed, by more than just her lack of sleep. We had to get on with the day, and she went upstairs to check the house phone for messages and take a shower. The phone had rung upstairs while we were talking. She soon came downstairs excitedly. Matt, the man who Jon had told us had also seen a White Sasquatch at the Quabbin, had left a message that he was trying to reach us. Donna immediately called him back.

Matt answered, and on speaker-phone we began an animated conversation. He and she were both obviously delighted to be confirming each other's experience. Seeing may be believing, but seeing something like a White Sasquatch is enough to make anyone doubt their grip on reality. Matt was well spoken and sounded entirely reasonable. Recently retired from the police force, he was an experienced outdoorsman and someone who seemed trained to be carefully observant. The conversation went on for the better part of an hour as Donna and I sat there fascinated by his story and astonished by his many similar experiences.

Surprisingly, his encounter involved much more than the recent sighting that had occurred only a few miles from where Donna and I had been on September 22, 2014. That had been a Monday; Matt's story began on the Friday before, September 19, 2014. He was camping by himself in the Green Mountains of Vermont, long before he had actually seen a creature. Hence, his ongoing encounter, like ours and like Jon's, was not isolated to one particular location and even included some very bizarre events that had happened at his home in Chicopee. All three of us were excited and amazed by the similarities in our experience, and when we suggested to Matt that we'd love to get together, perhaps at the Pelham house where we could show him the stick structure out in the woods, he asked if he could come right over. We both thought it was a great idea. I decided to postpone the project I was doing. This meeting seemed too important to delay. One of the strangest similarities between Donna's and my experience and Matt's was a loud noise that had happened in his house at about the same time that Donna heard the mysterious crash downstairs. What Matt and his wife had heard sounded to them like a "heavy piece of metal wrapped in plastic thrown with force against the wall of their bedroom." Again, whatever made the noise was invisible and nothing was out of place or fallen over in the room.

Matt's story

Matt had camped out in the Green Mountains of Vermont on the third weekend of September last year, just before Donna's sighting. He frequently went camping by himself, spending a weekend hiking by day and reading or playing guitar by the fire at night. He loved the peace and quiet. On this weekend, he'd found a secluded campsite on Glastenbury Mountain in Vermont. There are several campsites in the area, maintained by the state but available free of charge. On Friday evening, as Matt was setting up his tent and preparing the site, he felt strangely uneasy. Exploring the immediate area, he had found an odd structure of branches woven together and leaned against a tree, about ten feet tall and obviously placed there intentionally but serving no purpose he could imagine. As the light faded and he hastened to gather firewood, he became fearful and felt that someone or something was watching him from the darkness of the forest. He had camped out frequently without the slightest concern and could not account for his feelings, but he restricted his wood gathering to areas close to his tent. The night passed without incident, then he hiked the following day but again felt uneasy as night approached. Several times he heard the sound of someone knocking on a tree close by but saw and heard nothing else to suggest that people were near. He settled in for the night, cooking some food and reading by the fire. Three times, he heard the high-pitched barks and howls of coyotes passing through the forest close to the clearing where he was camped. It seemed odd that they would pass the same way several times in succession and unlikely that more than one pack was in the area.

He continued reading. Suddenly, a loud deep grunt came from just beyond the firelight, a sound that scared him so that he bolted for his truck, jumped in and slammed the door behind him. He had seen nothing and, scanning the area with a flashlight from the safety of the truck, still saw nothing. He decided he must have been imagining things and went back to his tent to turn in.

At some point after midnight, Matt woke up, overcome by a terror he didn't understand. Again, he raced to the safety of the truck. If he hadn't been unwilling to abandon his tent and gear, he would have driven away in the dead of night. He spent the remaining hours of darkness uncomfortably in the truck, then with the first light of day, packed up and headed for home.

Confused by his experience, he had looked into the history of Glastenbury Mountain and found that several people over the years had reported Bigfoot sightings. So began his interest in the subject. Moreover, Glastenbury Mountain was the center of an area sometimes known in local folklore as the Bennington Triangle. Two townships that had viable economies in the nineteenth century, Glastenbury and Somerset, had been largely abandoned as logging operations and mills shut down. The towns were officially unincorporated in 1937, and the little villages sank back into the forest, marked only by old foundations and stone walls like those settlements in the Quabbin watershed.

The folklore of the Bennington Triangle is grounded in one indisputable and very strange fact. Between 1945 and 1950, five people, three of them hikers, mysteriously disappeared. All three of the hikers had been with companions but disappeared after being briefly out of sight. One, a Bennington College sophomore, was seen by a couple walking behind her on the same trail. She went round a turn in the path, and when the couple came to the same spot, she was nowhere in view. The final disappearance was that of a woman who had left a family campsite on Somerset Reservoir to hike with a cousin. She had slipped and fallen into some water shortly after departing and decided to return to camp for dry clothes. She told her companion she would catch up to him. She never showed up at the camp and was never seen again. As in all these disappearances, an extensive search was carried out, but no trace of her was found till seven months later. The following May her body was found near the reservoir in an area that had been searched thoroughly after she disappeared. There was no way of telling from her remains what had been the cause of death. None of the other people who disappeared were ever found. Since the nineteenth century, there have been reports in this area of a creature matching the description of Bigfoot, known locally as the Bennington Monster, so associating the creature with the disappearances is easy to understand.

However fearful Matt had been up there on Glastenbury Mountain, his curiosity about the subject of Sasquatch in New England would not abate. He read up on the subject, encountered Jon Wilk, and learned that there had been sightings in the Quabbin. He started frequenting the area, and on a hike in May, 2015, he saw the creature, unless of course he only saw some phantasm of the mind. He was walking with his dog on one of the straight, wide trails, only a few miles from Donna's sighting, his eyes scanning from left to right, when suddenly he stopped short. He had seen a *white Sasquatch* standing off on the edge of the forest, about seventy yards ahead of him, its face partly obscured by branches, but staring directly at him. His eyes had passed over it before the image fully registered.

He looked back and it was gone. He questioned what he had seen. Was he imagining it? He had heard a wood knock shortly before the sighting. Had he imagined that? His dog had not reacted at all. He continued walking and soon reached the spot where he believed the creature had been standing. He could tell that it had to have been very tall. He kept questioning himself. Had he really seen what he thought he had seen? He asked out loud for a sign, some kind of confirmation, and promptly heard two loud wood knocks. At that point, Matt suddenly became very dizzy and disoriented and felt as if he might fall down. His head cleared after few moments and he continued on, somewhat unsteadily, back to the trailhead, astonished but unable to dismiss what he had seen as some trick of the mind.

One thing stood out in his description. The creature was a very clean, brilliant white, more so than would have seemed possible for such a being. A dirty white would be easier to understand for any animal living in the forest presumably in contact with leaves and dirt. This odd detail exactly matched Donna's description and was hard to account for as the product of an overactive imagination. It was not a detail he could have known about her sighting, as she had told no one except me. His reaction was also similar; like her, he was fascinated but not afraid of what he saw, in spite of the strange terror he had felt on Glastenbury Mountain and the odd dizziness after his sighting. I could not imagine having such a calm reaction had I found myself alone in the forest, locking eyes with such a being.

Matt arrived within the hour. He was younger than we'd imagined and obviously fit, someone we could easily imagine at ease traipsing through the forest and camping out far from the comforts of home. We immediately set out for the odd stick structure Donna had found in the woods out back. If not as big as the one at the Quabbin, it is impressive nonetheless. Though not something humans would have had difficulty building, the structure is strange indeed. It is bigger than anything young children could have built, yet too dysfunctional to have been some Boy Scout project. If it had been intended as the framework of a lean-to, the ground within it would not have contained a strange low pile of rocks. Matt had seen other odd configurations of branches and tree trunks in the woods but none quite as impressive. He was even more inclined than us to attribute this oddity to Bigfoot. The visit was brief, since I had to leave for an appointment at 4 PM and Matt had to meet his wife. I had the sense that it was important for all of us to meet in person, if only to reassure ourselves that these common experiences were indeed happening.

June 27

I'm back at my room in Northampton, just having a very slow evening by choice, resting for a change. It is peaceful here off from the center of town on a side street that runs down into the meadows, the long stretch of fields and swampy forest in the lowlands by the Connecticut River. There are certainly creatures wild enough to amuse, like the black bear that wandered into the alley behind a pizza shop a couple of years back and foraged in the Dumpster. I don't expect to see any two-legged hairy primates striding through the neighborhood though. I've sometimes felt myself succumbing to the strangeness of this whole adventure and, like Donna, have had to pull back from attributing every odd coincidence to some mysterious power emanating from the realm of the Squatch. Where is this all leading? At what point could we draw some meaningful conclusions? From the similarities between Matt's experiences and ours, the numerous similar accounts we seemed to always discover after each new bizarre occurrence, I cannot escape the feeling that there is some significant message embedded in these events.

July 2015

July 1

Several things to report. Out by her chair this past Saturday, Donna noticed another of the mysterious blue stones that appear periodically – not quite as blue as the others, but looking out of place. Are these something that occur naturally? Do they have any significance as "gifts"?

Donna had dinner with me at my place in Northampton last night, but went home before dark. She called shortly after she got home to tell me that when she stepped out of the car she heard a short howl from the woods, a sound she said was definitely not like a coyote or any other animal she could recognize. When I arrived here in Pelham today, she was still in her pajamas. She had not slept well. She says that at about 4 AM, she woke to hear an elongated howl coming from off in the forest, again, unlike any animal she might recognize but exactly like purported Sasquatch vocalizations we have heard online. She couldn't get back to sleep, not because the howl itself was troubling, but because she kept thinking about all the changes and decisions looming, where to live in the fall, how best to start up her business, etc. Matt is coming over at about 1 PM. I feel like I'm part of a support group, "Sasquatchers Anonymous." "Good evening, everyone. My name is John and I believe in Bigfoot."

Matt arrived as planned and he reiterated the story of his ongoing encounter. What stood out was his belief that so much communication was passing between him and the White Sasquatch. He and his wife had heard strange noises in his house, the unexplained crashing sound when nothing visible had fallen over, a sudden knock on the outside wall, just where the head of their bed is. Like us, he was coming to accept the strangeness of the experience.

There were just too many "coincidences." These he interpreted as oblique communications, as did I and Donna, but more than me, he felt a kind of benevolent intimacy in all of this, a reaching out from the creature as if to say, "Yes, I am real and have powers that you can barely imagine." Donna and he were both particularly animated by that sense of relief that comes from sharing an experience that disrupts your normal view of the world and makes you question your sanity. I realize that for all my involvement in this bizarre adventure, their experience is qualitatively different from mine. They both **saw** the White Sasquatch. We are such visual beings that an actual sighting has to have a much greater impact than just being witness to an accumulating series of corroborating events; even the unimaginable sounds that have so unnerved me cannot compare to seeing the creature. I have the sense that the sighting came to both of them as a profound shock, that they have both been changed in ways I may not understand.

July 5

On Friday, July 3rd, Donna and I walked again back to Gate 3A, where the White Sasquatch had first appeared, via Gate 4, as we did that time when we heard the loud whistling. The woods, though beautiful, seemed ordinary, the water duller under an ambiguous sky, the blue washed out behind thin clouds. Now, Sunday morning, I am writing reluctantly, out of a sense of duty to this journal. My notion of some wondrous creature, mysteriously free from the clutches of modern man, has been dulled, not enhanced, by the stranger events. It sometimes seems as if this whole experience has become a disturbing muddle of enigmatic occurrences: Cryptozoology meets table-rapping spiritualism, anthropology, and UFO research. Maybe I am just disturbed by the prospect that each of these endeavors could actually shine some light on reality. It is tiring to keep your grip on the world adrift in a sea of such complexities. At any rate, as we were both sitting by the water, somewhat grumpily, my cell phone rang. It was Matt.

He and his wife had been planning a weekend of camping up in the Adirondacks, but his wife had gotten sick, and they'd had to cancel their plans. Matt was bummed and concerned about his wife, but he wanted to share this story. Several weeks back, on one of his walks in the forest, during which he had felt the presence of the creature, he had found a particularly beautiful blue jay feather lying on the path. He had picked it up and carried it with him for a while. He imagined himself communicating with his invisible companion, even speaking out loud from time to time, a very opposite approach to that of the typical Sasquatch researcher who goes off howling and knocking on trees. When he started to head back to his car, he decided to leave the feather in the woods as a token of friendship. After all, such little "gifts" seem to be part of the friendly communication process that so many people are beginning to believe in.

As we both listened to Matt's story on speakerphone, I could see Donna's mood improving. Resigned to a very quiet weekend at home, he had been watching a movie in his living room. At some point when he took his eyes off the screen, he was startled to see a pretty blue jay feather sticking into an old Afghan spread over the couch. He is sure he left the feather in the forest and cannot imagine how it or one like it could have ended up where it did, even if he had somehow kept it in one of his pockets.

July 7

Yesterday, out of the blue, I got a call from David, my old guitar player. He had recalled an incident that had happened to him and our mutual friend Scott, the guitarist in Max Creek. This was years ago when we all lived in Connecticut. David and Scott had discovered a new road. It must have been work done to prepare for some new suburban development, and it wound its way up one of the high forested ridges that in those days still had no houses on them. The road simply stopped at a paved circle. The place had a great view, and they used to hang out there sometimes, smoking a joint.

One time when they were thus engaged, they were both suddenly overcome with uncontrollable terror. They did not say a word; they just looked at each other with wide eyes while Scott turned the key and they tore down the mountain as if the Devil Himself were chasing them. They never returned to that spot and never could explain the sudden blinding fear that had overcome them. Pot-induced paranoia? A 'Squatch nearby "vibing" intruders away from his territory, trying to guard the forest from development? The angry ghosts of Native Americans rumored to be buried nearby? I told David that I had reason to believe a White Sasquatch was in the vicinity where I had spent most of the last year and that I had once experienced an overpowering, unexplained fear that I thought might have been related. David replied, "Those tall thin white ones. They're vegetarians and I really think they're actually aliens."

Here we go again, down the rabbit hole.

July 10

I have a few more oddities to record. I have no conviction that they are related. Tuesday night, as I was getting in my car to head back to Northampton from Pelham, I heard the sound of someone dropping a garbage bag into one of the plastic cans that are lined up by the road, then the sound of the lid being snapped down. The landlord has rigged up a contraption to keep the varmints out, a wooden frame with chicken wire stretched across it that fits over the three cans and is held down by a long pole suspended from the trees above. The lids of the cans are themselves strapped down by bungee cords. There are plenty of creatures who would raid the garbage on a nightly basis were it not so difficult to get at.

What I heard was as distinct and familiar as any humdrum household noise – the thud and clink of trash dropping into the barrel and the lid being put back on – and it definitely came from the right location. I was standing by my car, at most thirty feet away, with a clear view of the chicken-wire contraption and tops of the cans. It was dark, but there was plenty of ambient light coming from the front door lantern. I had looked up when I heard the sound, but no one was there. I became somewhat alarmed, afraid actually, and I cried out, "Donna!" She was standing in the doorway looking towards the garbage cans.

At the same time, she called out to our neighbor and landlord, "Is that you, Andre?"

She expected to see someone on the road, but there was no one there, or hear footsteps or the rustling of some creature scurrying away. Donna went into the house, got a flashlight, and came back out. When we reached the garbage cans, everything was in place, the long pole firmly hooked over the chicken-wire frame. We have not been able to imagine what could have made the noise we heard. A creature scrambling over the chicken wire would not have sounded the same way, would not have recreated so accurately such a familiar sound.

Now, just after reading this to Donna, she tells me that the noise lasted longer than I remember, at least for her, that she heard it, called out to our landlord, got no answer, then went into the house to get her headlamp but did not see the light on the table; she went back out, still heard the noise, so she again went inside, got her flashlight upstairs and came out again. When she came out the second time, that's when she called out, "Who's there?" as we both walked towards the cans from opposite directions. By then, the sound had stopped and we saw no one. It was at that point that we examined the whole area and saw everything closed up tight. Hearing her account, and knowing her habit of precise observation and her detailed memory, I think her description the more accurate. Whatever minor discrepancies there are, we both clearly heard a sound we could only attribute to a person, yet saw no one, the sound of someone dropping a garbage bag into the garbage can and then snapping down the lid. Of course, we can always go back down the rabbit hole to retrieve an answer to the mystery. A hungry Sasquatch could have simply made himself invisible while rummaging about for some snack. All joking aside, I wonder why our separate recollections of the time that elapsed during this incident are so different.

July 11

Matt called yesterday, and we talked to him and spoke with his wife Sherri for the first time. She certainly had indeed heard those same strange sounds Matt had described. Matt was particularly excited because he had seen pictures of tree structures that closely resembled the one in the forest behind us, structures that some believe are markers for Sasquatch burials. Some members of a Facebook discussion group evidently believe that the burials are exceedingly deep, a likely excuse for their not revealing any bones, I thought. Indisputably, there are some very big and mysterious teepee structures of uncut wood, but burial markers? That does not seem in keeping with such a secretive creature, even if we accept the possibility of burials at all. Of course, if one took this idea seriously, it would be a simple matter to solve the mystery. I, for one, am oddly convinced that disturbing a Sasquatch burial site, if such a thing exists, is a bad idea and something I want no part of.

Matt also wanted to report two peculiar occurrences. He said he had felt someone touch his shoulder at some point during the previous day when there was no one there. Sherri had had a similar experience; something unexpectedly had brushed her hair aside as if some invisible hand had touched her affectionately. Sherri, like Matt, seemed glad to have someone to talk to about the experiences they were having. Matt also elaborated on something I had not fully understood about his own ongoing encounter. He had said once that on one of his walks, he had been startled by a very loud noise that he described as a "freight train coming through the woods." Since we were now on the subject of strange noises, he explained that he meant to convey what it was like to hear a very big tree falling in the forest, crashing through the surrounding growth and hitting the ground. Donna and I of course recalled the falling tree we had heard crash somewhere behind us as we were leaving the forest on that same day when we discovered the mysteriously broken tree that blocked the road into the Quabbin. Like us, Matt had seen no disturbance in the air, no dust or leaves swirling about or rebounding branches. He also observed that he had not felt the ground vibrate the way he would have expected given the volume and proximity of the sound.

I do not remember sensing any vibration.. I just recall how startled I was that a big tree or part of a tree was suddenly falling down near us, particularly on a day when there was no noticeable wind moving through the forest. Curiously, I was not particularly alarmed. In my years doing chainsaw work, I had become wary of falling timber or the possibility of a very large section of a rotten tree coming down unexpectedly. Donna, however, had been uneasy and had heard in her mind those words, "You're not out of the woods, yet." I do remember that as we neared the car, I imagined a Sasquatch pushing over a large dead tree as a way of sending us a warning. When we reached the tree that had been pulled down over the road and I had to jump out of the car to pull it aside, I was anxious to get back in as soon as possible. I am reminded of that old philosophical puzzle: If a tree falls in the forest and no one is around to hear it, does it make a sound? But how do we answer another question: If we hear a tree falling in the forest but no tree actually falls, did we really hear the sound of a tree falling?

July 15

I returned to Northampton later in the evening and called Matt to say that I would be too busy Thursday to do any hiking. We ended up talking for a while. He was anxious to make me understand better some of the experiences he had tried to describe before.

He and Jon Wilk had surmised that they had upset the creature or creatures by exploring their forest. When they had been looking at what they believed to be tree structures, some object had struck a tree next to which Matt was standing. Then, there had been that massive tree-crashing sound, and a couple of nights later, something had slapped the outside of Matt's house, just by the headboard of his bed. Jon and he went back to Gate 10, hoping to communicate their friendly intentions. They walked into the forest, actually talking out loud and apologizing. Jon whooped, as if trying to draw attention so their apologies would not go unnoticed. Suddenly, he spun around, bent over, and started vomiting. He felt a sudden panic and insisted that they leave the forest immediately. Matt felt confusion, some dizziness and nausea too. He said that it was as if a pulse had passed through him. He reminded me that earlier this spring, when he had seen the White Sasquatch, he had a similar experience. He had continued along the trail, in a sort of daze, questioning whether or not he was seeing things. When he reached the spot where he had seen the creature, he had felt that same dizziness and nausea. Later that day, he had had a severe headache that lasted for hours. Matt speculated that maybe he and Jon had felt the effects of the infrasound that some believe a Sasquatch can project.

As we were talking, Matt suddenly caught his breath. "Hey, wait a minute. Something strange just happened. I'm sitting on my back porch. A shadow just crossed the yard. I thought I saw the outline of a head and shoulders." What could we say? It was useless to speculate on whether or not some real being had just passed through the darkness. How could we tell? Donna had called and Matt seemed a bit uneasy, so we ended the conversation, agreeing to get together the following week.

I returned Donna's call. She was excited. Again, she had heard a mysterious tapping coming from the back yard. She had not been afraid, and she had gone to the window and looked out but could see nothing but the dark shapes of the nearest trees. It had been another rhythmic pattern, one that kept time, but not the same four-measure phrase she had heard before. When I didn't answer her first call, she assumed that I was talking to Matt. She also said she "knew that something was happening at Matt's." She told me that when I had not answered, she had written me an email describing what had just happened but had not yet sent it. Then, just as she finished the email, she heard a whoop.

There is something else I should mention. Both Matt and Donna have taken to calling the White Sasquatch Luke. Before I knew Donna, she had a boyfriend named Mark who had a close friend named Butch. Butch had evidently believed that there were Sasquatch at the Quabbin, an idea that Donna thought completely ridiculous. Butch had gone so far as to place a trail camera somewhere in the forest where he thought he could catch one on video. Donna had laughed at him but had been surprised that Mark would not join her in making fun of Butch. Somehow, Mark's involvement with Donna's first encounter with the subject triggered an association in her mind. This story about a White Sasquatch had its John (me), and its Matthew and less directly, Mark. Throw in Luke and what do you have but Matthew, Mark, Luke and John? Donna's background in the church and Bible studies kicked in and the name "Luke" popped into her mind. I don't want to read too much into it, but there did seem some resonance to the name, some suggestion that the White Sasquatch was the bearer of an important message, a figure whose very presence was a revelation of hidden, spiritual realities, a being who seemed to fill the void Donna had felt as she confronted egos and power struggles within the church.

Maybe, the Sasquatch, the wild man of the woods, was in some way the counterpart of her lost Jesus,

a pure being, not detached from the world but so at home that he could walk barefoot through the snow. "Adam raised a Caine," goes the old song. What really surprised me was how readily Matt took to the name. To both of them, the White Sasquatch became Luke, a personality, mysterious and immensely powerful but ultimately benign.

July 16

No outward manifestations today. Donna and I spent a large part of the day dealing with the house – what to do about her impending move in September. Matt called while we were discussing these issues. He wanted to know about our schedule. When could we take a walk? He'll be hiking in the Catskills this weekend, so it looks like next week some time will be our first opportunity to get together. While the three of us were talking, somehow, the subject of the 3/3/7 clacking noise came up and how Donna had heard the sound outside on the night I was playing with Max Creek. We talked about the song "Old Stones, Broken Bones," and Matt thought he had heard it. He knew about Max Creek and actually had had one of their recordings. To my surprise, Matt asked in all seriousness if we thought the Sasquatch was tapping out the rhythm of the song. The idea had never occurred to us, but as I thought about the rhythmic pattern, 123 rest,123 rest,1234, 123 rest, I was astonished to realize that this is exactly the same as the basic riff of the song. What were the chances, particularly since the rhythmic clacking had started at just about the time I stepped up to the microphone with the band pounding out that very rhythm behind me? How completely bizarre! The whole episode had been emotionally freighted because I was a last-minute addition to the lineup and could not get Donna a guest pass. The production company had allotted a certain number and even the Creek, the festival headliners themselves, couldn't get any more.

What the hell was this all about? I try to dismiss this as just another coincidence, but I've written a lot of songs and only one has that pattern. Moreover, it really defines the tune!

Yesterday was the day Donna made the final decision to leave the house in Pelham by September. We are both conflicted about this. There are problems with the house and even if I we lived together again it would still be too expensive and a little inconvenient. Maybe we both know instinctively that we can't get on with whatever comes next without making a move. It is so odd that this whole Sasquatch experience plays so strongly into our thinking about where to live. The allure of the mystery and the beauty of the forest seem to have held us in a kind of spell. But the world moves on. I feel that I have been so distracted by this endless series of peculiar events and unsolvable riddles that I really do need a change, however sad I may be that this chapter is coming to an end.

July 17

Today, when we least expected it, when I was beginning to think of this whole encounter as a story that was receding into the past where I could view it from a safe distance, Donna and I witnessed an extraordinary demonstration of strength, one we could only attribute to Luke or some other Sasquatch who wanted to make his or her presence known to us.

At about 5 PM, we hiked down the trail from Gate 16, a route we'd never taken before, but one that in about half a mile reached the water at a place on the shore where the westernmost branch of the lake narrows to its northern tip. The land on the eastern side of that tip forms the northern boundary of the Prescott Peninsula, an area off limits to hikers and fishermen. We had heard from a birdwatcher we met on a hike to a great blue heron nesting area that this stretch of shoreline harbored some very fruitful cranberry bushes. A short walk to a new destination with the prospect of locating some good cranberries for picking later in the year seemed like a fine way to end the day.

We came out to the typical stony beach. A small island lay close at hand and beyond that, a widening expanse of open water stretched south, bordered by hills and forest, a gradient of shades from the dark green of a nearby pine forest to the pale blue of the farthest shore. In all this expanse of water and woods, there was no sign of human activity. Even with my powerful binoculars, we could see no boat or fisherman on the shore. Only the stone tower many miles away dispelled the illusion that we had entered some uninhabited landscape. It was also quiet. I briefly heard a few crows chattering somewhere on the opposite shore, but they were soon gone, and it was still again.

We headed north, in the direction of those cranberry bushes we'd been told about, taking our time. There was plenty of daylight left; we were both a little tired and felt no need to hurry along. Up ahead, we could see what looked like the northern limit of the water and a green stretch of shoreline that I thought might be those cranberry bushes. We did notice an odd stick structure right on the shore. It looked like a low lean-to, two vertical sticks with rocks at their base and some haphazard branches leaned against a cross piece. I thought maybe some fisherman had built it for shade, though it was too low to sit in comfortably and had only one evergreen bow over the top, not much in the way of shade. Donna was more interested than I, implicitly wondering if this might not be something other than the work of a human being. Neither of us bothered to take a picture. We were looking for birds and cranberry bushes, not Bigfoot. Just yards off shore, the clear water darkened into a deep channel and I was musing about taking a dip, something I've never done there. *What would be the harm?* I thought. *There doesn't seem to be anyone within miles. I know it's illegal but...*

Just as I was entertaining the idea of plunging into the lake, something caught my eye, some dark object in the air arcing down. We both saw a big splash about thirty yards off shore and heard the loud deep "thunk" of a very large rock hitting the water. The sound was unmistakable. This was no beaver tail or jumping fish. Someone had hurled a very heavy stone into the water, someone or some being standing in the trees above the shore, just yards ahead of us. The amount and direction of the displaced water made this clear. The object hurled out of the forest was obviously something much heavier and bigger than anything a human being could throw such a distance.

We looked at each other with astonishment and a little annoyance. We weren't looking for Bigfoot today. We were taking a stroll along a beautiful shore, exploring for cranberry bushes. This was *our* place, a landscape where we could escape the pressures and uncertainties of our lives, even of our own relationship. Perhaps the odd events I have been describing in recent pages had left me somewhat fatigued by the whole experience, exasperated by my inability to make sense out of what was happening. The big hairy ape had become a magician and mind reader, a creature more of the spirit world. Now here he was again behaving just like...well...a big hairy ape. Neither of us was particularly scared, but we knew immediately that our evening walk was now cancelled. There was no way we would continue along that shoreline. We had no doubt as to what had happened.

Rock-throwing has been described by Bigfoot experiencers, most often as a kind of threat display, though sometimes as an actual act of violence. There is the famous Ape Canyon incident from the 1920s in Washington State; a group of miners were barricaded all night in their cabin while Sasquatch supposedly bombarded them with large stones. The men were convinced that, had they not been able to return rifle fire, they would never have survived.

Donna and I briefly conferred, and to both of us, it was obvious that a boulder had been hurled where we could not fail to see and hear its impact on the surface of the lake. This did not seem like a friendly hello. We turned and walked quickly to the trail's outlet and back through the forest to the car. Nothing else unusual happened, though I remember the woods as very quiet. During the whole walk we had seen no birds and only heard those crows briefly on the far shore.

Since our hike had been cancelled and we still had plenty of daylight left, we drove to a nearby town to look for a small state park that supposedly contained a good swimming spot. We found the place easily and saw a few parked cars. Two short trails led to a large pond, the far reaches of which transitioned into a boggy area unsuitable for swimming, but looking like a great habitat for wildlife. We followed a trail to the opposite end where there was open water and a small beach. The cooler air of evening made the idea of a swim unappealing, but we were happy to find a place to head to the next time the weather turned hot. I noticed a number of rocks near the outlet of the pond where a stream descended into a steep gully. We were still thinking about that big stone dropping in the reservoir thirty yards from shore. Did that really happen? Was that object that hit the water as big as we thought it was? I picked up the heaviest stone I could find that was still light enough for me to throw with two hands. I hurled it as far as I could into the deepest spot I could see. It only went a few yards, and the splash it made was small and lacked the force of what we had seen on our hike. It lacked also the lower-pitched sound of a dense, very heavy object plummeting into deep water. We cannot imagine any possible explanation except that we had come very close to a Sasquatch. Nothing else exists that can throw a heavy stone such a distance.

As we drove back to Donna's that evening, she wondered out loud, "What if that rock was not a warning? What if was a way of letting us know he was there, he was real. What if it was an invitation? What would have happened if we had continued along that shore? Would we have seen him face to face?" I knew I would not have had the courage to keep walking along that shore, and I doubted very much that that rock had been meant as an invitation, at least not as an invitation to *me*.

Even after all we've been through, we both have a hard time believing that Luke or one of his kind was standing nearby, observing our approach, poised to announce his presence with a display of superhuman strength, but we can find no logical alternative. We are also acutely aware of how absurd this story might sound to someone unfamiliar with the subject and skeptical about the creature's very existence. Although this occurrence was among the least ambiguous we have experienced, the evidence of its happening at all disappeared with the last ripple on the water. Donna noted later in the evening that she had already begun to feel disconnected from what had happened. Yes, such a dramatic display was most certainly a kind of communication, but somehow it was impersonal, lacking in the subtle psychological dimension that seemed a part of our earlier encounters. There was nothing else in the event that hinted directly at the presence of a large animal, no sound of footsteps or moving brush, no smells or vocalizations of any kind. Even if our creature was standing further back than the arc of the stone had indicated, it seems impossible that something, anyone big and strong enough to have thrown such an object, could have done so without creating some disturbance.

July 23

I have put the rock-throwing incident out of my mind for the last few days. God knows I have other concerns, scrambling to pay some bills, getting a couple of small jobs done, trying to decide how best to use some recording time and line up more gigs like those I did this spring. Not to mention figuring out where I will be in the fall. Back with Donna yesterday, talking through a number of issues, I found myself overcome with fatigue. I settled back on the couch for a few minutes and briefly nodded off. She might not have even noticed had I not suddenly jerked convulsively. I had slipped into a dream in which, with great effort, I was attempting to heave a large stone into the lake, spinning around sideways as I lifted the stone with two hands and released it. It was as if my subconscious would not let me ignore the significance of what had happened. But what really was that significance, if only to the two of us?

Last night I stayed with Donna and woke before dawn with another dream drifting out of memory, vague images of shadowy figures disappearing among misty trees. More than the figures themselves, I could recall the feeling of the mist on my skin, the cool fog that shrouds the forest on early autumn mornings. I lay there while the images faded, remembering the sudden splash of the boulder and the deep resonance of its impact. Maybe that stone had something to do with our both knowing that it was time to move on, that we could not let ourselves be overwhelmed by contradictions we could never resolve. What we had experienced was as real as that rock hitting the water or that young tree pulled over by some unknown force, but we had to focus our attention on those realms of life we better understood. We had to suspend our belief, not our disbelief.

The acclaimed naturalist and writer Robert Pyle in 1995 wrote a serious enquiry into the Bigfoot phenomenon, *Where Bigfoot Walks: Crossing the Dark Divide*. He wrote, "Bukwus and Dzonoqua (native terms for male and female Sasquatch) probably haven't stolen any children lately, *but they still steal souls*. I have known good men to give up their jobs, families and reputations to go in search of the big-footed ones." This is not a pattern either Donna or I wish to emulate. Pyle also reminds us that Native Americans who know the woods better than anyone else believe Bigfoot to be real. They also fear the creature and seem to acknowledge its paradoxical nature as guardian of the forest, a being who is at once benevolent and dangerous, flesh and blood, yet magical, endowed with abilities we don't understand. Pyle's book about his trek into the Dark Divide – an area framed by the five largest peaks in Washington State – is full of vivid descriptions of the scenery from which some of the better-known Bigfoot tales have emerged, but he only discovers tantalizing shreds of evidence. Strangely, we, here in an area vastly more populated than the northwest wilderness, have come much closer to the creature, unless, of course, Pyle was being secretly observed. We seem to have entered our own dark divide, one not framed by mountains, but by the limits of our understanding. What can we conclude as we stare into this wilderness of the unknown, knowing that we must integrate our day-to-day lives into a society that barely acknowledges the wonder of the humblest creature, much less the existence of an impossibly secretive giant, a monster out of mythology lurking in our back yard?

July 26

This past Friday, Matt met us in Pelham and we went to Gate 16. The day was beautiful and the walk uneventful. Somehow,

Donna and I both felt safer with a third person along. We hiked past the area where the rock had hit the water and found those cranberries our birder friend had described. The boggy ground was spread with the low plants and the green berries were every bit as plentiful as he had claimed. There were fresh moose tracks in the wet earth.

With our binoculars we could see a white spire that seemed to rise like a luminous tube of light out of the distant forest at the southern end of the peninsula to our east, quite a few miles away. We couldn't imagine what it was. It appeared large, almost as large as the distant stone tower we recognized. Was it sunlight hitting a large dead tree? We couldn't steady the image well enough to see for sure. There was no sign of our boulder hurling hominin. Matt thought he heard a wood knock but I did not. There are so many sounds in the woods, our imaginations can easily play tricks on us.

We returned to the car with plenty of daylight left and headed back down Route 202. Matt wanted to show us a couple of possible stick structures he had found with Jon Wilk. They were visible from the road, and I was skeptical about their being anything but random. However, there was one structure that was hard to attribute to chance. A forked stick, the kind of symmetrical Y shape people used to make sling shots out of, had been plunged into the ground. One end of a straight branch rested in the Y, the other on the ground. It was certainly odd. This putative structure had led Matt and Jon to explore the nearby trail on which Jon had been overcome by that sudden nausea and dizziness.

Back at the house, Donna and I uploaded the photos we had taken of the richly colored landscape. The white tower was there, appearing even more mysterious and luminous, emerging, it seemed, out of the distant forest. In one picture, within a large cumulus cloud directly above the white object, was a strange black shape looking very much like a disc. *What the devil is that?*, I thought, remembering all those tales associating Bigfoot with

UFOs. Enlarged to the max, the luminous white image seemed like a perfect rectangle. What have we here? A UFO beaming up our hairy friend to receive a report on the doings of the earthlings, or some mundane but pixilated object? In several of the photos, the position of the object seemed to move rather rapidly down the far coast. How could this be? Was this the result of our own changing position on the shore? That would be impossible if the object was as far away as it seemed, actually on that distant shore. I began to imagine that I had photographed some crazy phenomenon, Lord knows what, maybe one of those ill-defined vortices discussed by "researchers" of the paranormal. We laughed at such a notion but I could not dispel the idea that I had seen something unusual.

Late the following afternoon, Donna and I decided to return to that stretch of the shore from which we'd all observed the white mystery object. The day was cloudy but bright enough to see all the way down the west branch of the reservoir. When we got to the shore, I steadied the high-powered binoculars against a tree and saw quite clearly some kind of tall white marker, a warning about hidden rocks I guessed. We had been dazzled by the sunlight; even my camera had. The tall white object was obviously much closer, nowhere near that distant shore. Hence its position against the backdrop of the hills beyond had changed as we made our way around the curving beach. How easily our senses can fool us, I thought, a little disappointed if I'm honest about it. What of that dark shape within the cloud? I imagine there is some meteorological explanation.

We relaxed and enjoyed the soft wind that blew across the water. Three loons, parents and a chick I think, cruised up and down the central channel, diving and resurfacing, a couple of times with a fish clearly visible in the beak. We tried to calculate whence that big stone had been thrown. Donna had noted the exact spot we'd reached along the shore. I stood up on the bank at the first open space that offered any concealment and threw a much smaller stone to mimic the trajectory of that large rock. Whatever tricks the sunlight had played on our eyes Friday afternoon, we had no doubts about the size of that stone that had flown out of the woods the previous week or the strength it would have taken to hurl it to where it landed. As I stood there above the stony beach, I thought I heard a soft grunt somewhere behind me in the woods. I jumped down to the shore and turned nervously around. Of course there was nothing there.

Back near the trail's outlet, we sat on the mossy bank for a while as the loons made those occasional brief calls with which they seem to convey to each other some information about what they have found down in the dark water. A couple of wood thrushes and a bird I didn't recognize started singing somewhere back in the forest, so melodiously that I at first thought a musically gifted hiker was whistling his way happily down the trail. Off to my right, from somewhere deeper in the woods, I heard a sharp knock, like the sound of a baseball bat striking the ball full on. Wood knock? Who knows?

In the last week or so, there have been other anomalous events. Donna was just about to go to sleep on one of the nights when I was away when she heard what she describes as a sound like the jingling of keys at the bottom of the stairs. As has happened with other strange sounds, this occurrence evoked an immediate response from Chessi the cat. She leapt to investigate as did Donna, but nothing was there. This sound was very much like what Matt had heard in his bedroom right before he discovered the blue jay feather, a sound he thought was made by his dog's tags.

A couple of nights before that, when I was fast asleep in Pelham, Donna heard something slap the wall of the house. A few days prior to the wall slap, some creature screamed off in the woods, not a fisher cat, she says, but something that sounded more human. Matt just two days ago heard a couple of classic whoops in the cornfield beyond his house. He thinks, partly based on intuition alone, that it was a mother and a young one and that the mother may have been warning her child to stay well back from the road. Such occurrences are starting to be commonplace, not worthy of endless analysis. No doubt some of them have some mundane explanation, but all of them? One thing continues to stand out: As the encounter has unfolded, we have repeatedly experienced behaviors that we have subsequently found in accounts by others: wall slaps, rock throwing, nocturnal howling.

For some reason, I've neglected to tell about a dream I had last fall. I was sleeping in the Pelham house, in reality and in the dream itself. I knew that the great hairy man was in here too and that he was coming up the narrow 1790 staircase, then standing there hunched over on the landing, too tall for the height of the ceiling, breathing heavily, hesitating, it seemed, while I lay there, sheer terror rippling through my body. The door swung slowly open and his slightly crouched dark form, the silhouette of a shoulder and head, emerged into the pale moonlight that spilled in from the bedroom window. I woke up groaning, some kind of muffled scream twisting me up inside, but as I came to, the fear broke like a stretched rope. I was standing by the bed greeting the dark figure with an inexpressible joy, like a long-lost brother. My eyes opened and I found myself half out of bed, the covers thrown back, one foot on the floor and Donna groggily muttering, "What's going on?"

"I was dreaming of the Sasquatch," I replied, falling back into bed and sleeping soundly till morning. I remember that dream so vividly. Why now did I just write it down? And when exactly did I have that dream?

August 2015

August 3

This past Thursday, Matt called me when I was in Boston. One night last week, he had been out on his porch playing his guitar. He looked over to an area of tall grass and brush at the edge of his yard and thought he saw the dark shape of a head, a very thick neck, and wide shoulders drop out of sight. Thursday morning, he went out through the brush and found the area beaten down by something. He thought he saw impressions where a very large bipedal creature might have walked. He found two parallel pathways of pushed-over grass as if two beings had passed through the area in tandem, heading to the nearby farm field where he thinks he had heard two different cries. He imagines he might have heard a mother and child. Later that night, just before 4 AM, he heard voices whispering outside his bedroom window. They seemed to be conversing in some unfamiliar language. He is really intent on making contact and planned to sleep outside in a tent. I haven't spoken to him since.

This past Saturday, Donna found a pretty blue jay feather on the driveway right after Matt had told her about asking Luke for a blue jay feather. She placed it at the center of a small flat stone on the sill of the upstairs window with the blue side up to catch the sunlight. These feathers have a dark gray underside. At some point, she noticed that the feather, though still in the same position, had been flipped over so that the gray side was up. If a breeze had flipped it, it would have fallen off the small stone. Had I perhaps picked it up and looked at it? In fact, I hadn't even noticed it. The cat? Well, as she pondered how the feather might have flipped over but remained in the same position, the cat did jump up on the desk by that window, notice the feather, and knock it completely off the stone with her paw. The only way we can imagine turning over the feather is by picking it up between two fingers. Another significant coincidence, given the possible significance of a blue jay feather in this narrative. Donna had admittedly been reminded of Matt's story when she found the feather. Of course, there is little more one can say. Maybe the house has a mischievous spirit who wants to communicate.

August 8

I stayed in Pelham the last two nights. Our permanent departure was now just three weeks away. We had both been letting go for some time, but not without moments of misgiving and regret. I noticed when I intermittently returned to the house how dark it was during bright summer days compared to my room in Northampton. We recalled how during the long winter, with a bright fire and those small decorative Christmas bulbs strung across the dark hardwood beams, the little house had seemed like an island of light. Now in high summer, the cool shade that enveloped the house was somehow oppressive. Though our days here had been full of open skies and broad vistas as we hiked the reservoir shores, the house itself was confining and had drawn us inward. Our whole ongoing encounter still seemed to belong to this inward nocturnal world, regardless of the physical evidence we had seen in broad daylight. It was certainly true that we had both encountered parts of ourselves when we encountered the creature, but now we had to move on, back into some new chapter of our lives. The uncertainty about what lay ahead in our emotional and practical lives was much more unsettling than all the riddles posed by the White Sasquatch.

Donna had asked for another sign. I still don't really understand her need for some communication from the creature, something she shares with Matt. Maybe this is a condition that has something to do with their sightings, with the impact of actually seeing this being. She had wished out loud for a cardinal feather; she has always wanted a cardinal feather and has never found one. She found one today on the path to the car. It is tiny, a fan of gray down with a band of red across the top like a plume that might adorn the headdress of some South American shaman. Of course, cardinals are extremely common and neither of us would suggest that this discovery is a gift. Last night, however, shortly after we'd turned off the lights and had been wondering out loud whether or not we'd ever experience any further signs, we were startled by a loud slap on the wall next to the downstairs door. The stairway descends from a landing just outside the bedroom door to the narrow hallway just inside the front entrance. The bedroom door was open and the sound was clear and loud. It was the same sound Donna had heard months before, one that I could duplicate by slapping the outside wall with my open hand.

I am beginning to wonder whether or not there is an end to this story. Of course, true stories never end. Events echo infinitely outward like the proverbial ripple in the air caused by the butterfly's wing. But what will happen when neither Donna nor I live anywhere near the forest where these encounters have taken place? I sometimes think the story on these pages would have faded out of memory already had I not written it down, just the way the most intense dreams, happening as they do in what seems an alternate reality, elude us when we are awake. The loud whistling in the brush, the whooping noises I heard that night by the woodpile – even now, like dreams that fade out of memory, I recall them best when I read this account. But sometimes language falters. That whooping I heard in the forest, for instance. I remember its effect on me more than the sound itself. What was that sound? A hoot, a whistle, a scream, some combination of all those? What do we mean when we use the word "whoop"?

We went to the supermarket that evening, and Donna laughed at the way I wandered around in a daze, absolutely useless, staring vacantly at the tabloids by the checkout line. I remember how I felt, the stunned excitement, but the sound itself I cannot recreate in my head the way I can recall the voices of friends and family even if they've been gone for years, or other familiar noises. Perhaps the strangeness of the sound makes it a file without a folder, a memory we can't easily retrieve.

I suppose we often edit out of mind events that defy our everyday categories of experience even though we are attracted by their mystery. A friend of mine remarked recently that man's fascination with the unexplained is another aspect of the search for immortality. In glimpsing what lies beyond the known world, in this case the mythical giant who roams the forest in defiance of all our accumulated knowledge, we experience something like the ancient world of spirits and magical beings. And maybe this experience is not merely metaphorical. Maybe the creature we have encountered actually inhabits that world as well as our own, at least in the sense that it has powers we cannot explain.

Again and again, we are left with impossibilities, or at least contradictory observations. The Sasquatch must exist because he leaves identifiable traces: footprints that cannot have been faked, video and photographic images proven to be authentic, corroborating reports from witnesses unknown to each other, even hair, blood, and feces samples that defy known classifications. Yet, on the other hand, the Sasquatch can't exist. We have no bones, no specimen. And how could the largest creature in North America, other than a moose or grizzly bear, elude detection so successfully while foraging within walking distance of major universities and large towns? This ability to remain or quickly become invisible could be part of a cultural heritage, some kind of learned behavior, facilitated by amazing speed and grace and nocturnal habits. But what of the strange connection Donna` seems to feel towards the creature, the bizarre coincidences and emotions that cluster around the subject of these encounters? Is this simply the result of our fascination with a being at once so like us, and yet so different? Is it really evidence of some psychic field emanating from the creature, or an ability like the projection of infrasound, something we feel but cannot identify with our senses?

Donna's sighting last September cracked open our world, threw us both off course, in some ways drew us closer together but also underscored our differences. She was shocked to see something completely at odds with her own beliefs, but she was inexplicably overjoyed. I at first was scared but excited to see proof of what I had always believed was likely a real creature. However, as time went on and I began to suspect some kind of psychic connection, my rational mind felt frustrated. My white male, dominant-culture assumptions about reality were threatened. It was one thing to discover another wondrous creature on the evolutionary tree. It was quite another to imagine the hairy man-beast tapping out the rhythm of a song I was playing twenty-five miles away. The whole idea is ridiculous and downright funny. Then there was the improbability of certain events. How did I guess when Donna had just made up her mind to go back to Gate 3A, and how in the name of God did a Sasquatch or some other unknown creature manage to show up at that very moment right on our path and whistle at an almost unimaginable volume, this before either of us had any knowledge that whistling has been associated with the creature for centuries, as is evidenced by ancient ritual masks from northwest Indians showing a Sasquatch with pursed lips? Then there was the crashing tree and the more recent boulder, not to mention the various occurrences at the forest home. How could we possibly be having all these encounters without there being some connection, some conscious attempt at communication going all the way back to the creature's first showing himself to Donna? We weren't finding Bigfoot. Bigfoot was finding us. Even if half of these experiences had some other conventional explanation, something very weird was going on.

Our compatriot Matt has had a parallel run of apparent encounters. His experience on Glastenbury Mountain might have begun his unexpected journey and started him on the research that led to his sighting, but what of the strange goings-on at his house? Are they coincidental? The cries in the cornfield out back, the shadow streaking across his yard as we talked, the odd noises including slaps against the outside of his house. How can one person have encounters at completely different locations? By imagining things that are not real, of course, but I don't buy that. Why would different people imagine the same experiences *before* learning of these repeating motifs of purported Sasquatch behavior?

August 25

Tonight is our last night in the little house in the Pelham hills. Tomorrow, I'll pick up the cargo van and we'll start hauling out the last of the furniture. Donna has been lamenting the seeming lack of activity...she misses the excitement and the strange kind of enchantment that has marked our ongoing encounter. This evening, we dropped her car off at the local mechanic's for some brake work. As we were driving away, we noticed the slanting sun striking the passenger-side rear window at just the right angle to illuminate another large hand print, very similar to the previous ones, with an elongated palm the top of which seemed less curved than a human's. We stopped and walked over to her parked car. Looking at my own hand, I noticed how much shorter my palm was. If I drew a line along the base of each finger the line curved like the perimeter of a circle, much more so than in the print. I tried to make a print that looked the same but could not. It was very hot and I was sweaty from all the work of moving. My hand left a mark but there was no way I could produce a similar looking print or one as large. If I slid the heel of my hand along the glass to create the impression of that longer palm, I just created an indistinct smudge. There must have been a visitor last night. We were both tired and feeling a bit subdued. Was this really another message? Could some normal human have left the mark, someone with an oddly shaped hand? We couldn't say for sure, but whoever had left it had pressed their hand firmly against the window. Why would anyone do this accidentally if they were just opening a door or steadying themselves? The print suggested curiosity to me, as if someone had pressed a hand firmly against the glass in order to know what this transparent material felt like. Of course this gesture also made sense if someone was consciously trying to leave such a mark, if it *was* indeed a message. We took a couple of pictures and drove away. We still had many hours of packing ahead of us.

Last Thursday night, Donna was awake at about 4 AM when she heard a rock hit the outside wall of the house near the bedroom, then thump on the ground below. At least that's how she described the sound. When I got there the next afternoon, I found a rock just where one would have fallen if it had been thrown in such a way as to make that sound. There was even a mark on the clapboards above, where the paint had been chipped off.

Sometimes I worry that the White Sasquatch has threatened to become a white whale, dragging us down Ahab-like into depths of inexplicable and contradictory experiences. I've come to realize that this is the really strange part of the story, the part that escapes our normal categories of experience. Hence, we have a being at once primitive and potentially brutal, yet seemingly endowed with almost mystical powers, a creature smart enough to elude humans yet somehow driven to communicate with us if only to assure us of his existence.

I remain perplexed by the synchronistic encounters of the last year, how, against all odds, at different times and places, the creature has made his presence known: the sighting, the loud whistles when we returned weeks later, that hurled rock many miles north of the original encounter. It seems that our Sasquatch has known our whereabouts and made it a point to show up and remind us that he is still there.

I want to finish this story and get back to my other projects! Every time we think the whole episode is over, some new event occurs like this latest hand print. But we are leaving this place now, and maybe that hand print is a final wave good-bye from our mysterious companion.

I've come to suspect that we have encountered a creature sent to upend all of our complacencies. It is no surprise that we find him in a place where the natural world is rebounding. Where less than a century ago farms and small town businesses flourished, a great lake extends over two sunken valleys. Hills that rolled down to the Swift River now define an undulating shore overhung with tall pines. Eagles patrol the skies. By some cosmic irony, an environment created by man to supply water to the urban east coast has released the creative power of the wilderness, and from that reclaimed land a creature has emerged that defies our modern materialist arrogance. I cannot explain what we have experienced. I don't know that a Sasquatch is reading our minds, or senses our whereabouts even when we are miles away. I don't know whether through infrasound or some unknown manipulation of frequencies this being can affect our senses, project fear or calm or make himself invisible. If the genetic studies of Melba Ketchum have any merit and this being is part human and part something else, I cannot imagine what that something else might be. To me, however, the creature embodies a re-emergence of the sacred in nature, the spirit world, the unknowable. Perhaps, as most native traditions seem to intimate, Sasquatch is a very real creature, but one that can alternate between the solid world we walk through every day and some largely invisible dimension that we only visit in dreams or glimpse rarely when certain synchronicities occur or a shadow crosses the yard. Who are we to say that evolution can only develop capacities like those we recognize in ourselves?

I have no interest in being a Sasquatch researcher. I don't intend to go off howling in the forest and knocking on trees. I don't know whether the creature is some ice age relic, an offshoot of *Homo erectus*, Gigantopithecus, or some hybrid primate created by alien visitors. I no longer dismiss any possibility. Nor do I assume that this creature is entirely benign, at least insofar as my own very human hopes and fears are concerned. The natural world does not revolve around mankind, and its complexity will always ensure that unintended consequences will arise when we try to reduce creation to what we can control. I prefer the dangers of the wild unknown to a barren dying world where every aspect of creation is viewed as a commodity.

September 2015

September 22

On the one-year anniversary of Donna's sighting at the Quabbin, we decided to hike down the trails at Gates 16 and 3A, the two locations where our encounters had been unambiguous. We started early. The day was somewhat cloudy, not like the brilliant days of our former experiences at these spots. At the shoreline where the Gate 16 trail ends, a steady but gentle wind blew across the lake, filling the air with a cool sweetness. This time, we hiked past the cranberry bushes, all the way back to the narrow strait where the west branch terminates in a wide stretch of marshy ground. Here, the water curves around to the west, and steep wooded banks plunge almost to the water's edge.

Donna kept looking up the bank and feeling drawn toward the forest above, so we hauled ourselves up the incline and poked around. The area had been logged some years back and rotted tops and branches were strewn about. A number of small branches had been laid up against a tree, forming an odd, miniature teepee-like stick structure. Lying parallel next to each other on the ground in front of the little structure were more sticks. Someone had gathered a large number of these little branches and placed them in this peculiar configuration for no discernable reason. Of course, this was not far from where that boulder had been hurled back in July. Maybe this was some kind of Sasquatch creation, a symbolic structure, a hieroglyph of broken branches. Had some fisherman's child been playing here in the forest? I suppose it's possible. Unlikely, though, given the steep climb from the water's edge and the unappealing tangled landscape. We soon hiked back past those cranberry bushes and up the trail to the car. There had been no fishermen out on the water, no birds in the air or on the lake. It was the last day of summer, but it felt like fall had arrived already.

By the time we reached the water at Gate 3A, the day had clouded over more, but the steady breeze continued, and I had a momentary feeling of being at the ocean. We did not linger on the shore but headed back up the trail, pausing where Donna had seen the tall white figure passing behind trees. The brush had risen higher over this past year, and it was hard to know exactly which trees the creature had walked behind, though we could tell the approximate location from a large rock next to the trail. Neither of us had any sense of anything unusual today. This was not the enchanted forest it had seemed a year ago.

The oddest occurrence of the last week did not involve me at all. Over the weekend, Donna had taken a walk on Mt. Tom with Mark, her old boyfriend, a man who has been curious but skeptical about the existence of Sasquatch. Evidently, he had (in his mind) asked for a sign and jokingly noted that since he is a collector of rocks, perhaps a Sasquatch could leave him a nice specimen. Why not, if leaving gifts is supposed to be one of their habits? As he and Donna came round a corner on a trail that Mark knew well from previous hikes, there was the specimen he had wished for – a very large quartzite boulder he had never seen before, very large indeed, nothing that any person could have placed there and not the kind of rock a rock collector would have failed to notice. Moreover, it obstructed one side of the path and would not likely have been left there by park crews when the trail was built. Mark was quite confused by the presence of this boulder but certainly not ready to accept that it was the token he had wished for. Donna and he were left with the usual ambiguity. Perhaps he'd somehow managed to miss this stone on earlier hikes. That seemed odd but certainly not absurd, like the prospect of a psychic Sasquatch anticipating his location and retrieving for him an appealing geological specimen.

The day after our sighting anniversary, I had to postpone a trip
to New York, so Donna and I went to see that boulder on Mt Tom.
It occurred to me that we could tell if the boulder had in fact been
recently left there by examining the ground underneath. Would
lifting the stone reveal a dark impression such as one finds
underneath a rock pried up from the ground, or would the area look
like the rest of the path? When we reached the rock, I noticed
immediately how out of place it looked and dissimilar to other
stones in the area. I also could see no nearby impression from
which it might have been moved. It was bigger than I had expected.
I couldn't raise it off the ground even an inch. I finally knelt down
on the uphill side of the stone and pushed with all my strength. The
rock lifted slowly, then, as I pushed its top downhill, flipped over
once, landing heavily just below its original location. There were
leaves and bits of twigs where the stone had been lying, just as on
the rest of the path – no darkened patch of decomposed matter and
moist earth. The boulder had to have been placed there very
recently. Is that proof of more Sasquatch activity? Of course not.

Like so much of what had happened the previous year, the
presence of the boulder was another enigma. If it was a sign of the
mysterious giants, we would probably never know. I recognize that
even speculating about the possibility of such an occurrence sounds
absurd. Then I remember that the boulder's location is less than a
mile from where those two teenagers were terrified one night by a
roar so loud it scrambled their senses. This happened long before
Bigfoot had gained his current prominence in pop culture. Those
kids had no idea what had made the sound. I also recall that Jon
Wilk, who now works with the Bigfoot Researchers Organization,
told me that a father and son had recently reported seeing one of
the creatures on this very mountain. What am I to believe? Is this
all some form of mass hysteria? Is the archetype of the wild man
manifesting itself spontaneously in numerous people, breaking out
of the Jungian collective unconscious and even leaving traces in the

physical world? Are we experiencing some quantum effect, an example of the observer influencing that which is observed but in day-to-day experience, not in the realm of subatomic particles?

I started this journal imagining myself an amateur anthropologist. We had not traveled to some distant location to observe an unknown tribe or the behavior of one of our primate relatives. The remote wild place had come to *us*. The familiar landscape where I have lived most of my adult life was transformed and had become a newly discovered territory with secrets I could never have imagined.

After examining the strange boulder on the path and searching the surrounding forest for any explanation of its presence, Donna suggested we hike to Goat Peak, the summit of Mt Tom. Various hawks were now migrating south down the Appalachians, catching the thermal updrafts that rise up the flanks of the mountains from the warm lowlands. From the tower on Goat Peak, we would be able to see 360 degrees, surveying much of the countryside where we had spent the last year.

We reached the tower with plenty of time before the park gates would be closed. No hawks were immediately visible, but we could make out many landmarks. Off in the hills above the distant high-rise buildings of the University of Massachusetts, we could see the white dome of the Peace Pagoda, the Buddhist center next to my new rental in Leverett. Southeast of there was the fire tower in the Cadwell Forest on the highest hill near our old house, the tower Donna had taken me to when we were first getting to know each other; we had gone there often and surveyed the changing colors of the landscape. We had called that "tower time." Beyond in the same direction, we could make out the stone tower at Quabbin Park. I remembered looking out at that tower from the opposite shore just before we started back up the path towards the car and encountered the being whose presence had seemed to cast a spell over the last year, who had in fact led us to this very moment on a mountain top overlooking the Connecticut Valley. In every direction, the landscape was dominated by forest, more so than had been the case a hundred years ago, even with all the development and population growth. The tilted basalt summits of the Holyoke range rolled off east across the river, and villages I knew to the west were submerged in the hazy blue of the hills.

Suddenly, a kettle of hawks burst into view, eleven or twelve swept down from the north, spiraling upwards on the thermals, then breaking away and scattering as each bird balanced on the wind and coasted south. They were gone in an instant, out of sight so quickly it was impossible to find them with my binoculars.

What knowledge do the hawks possess to guide them south with such assurance? Is it "just instinct," whatever that reductionist term means? Maybe the more interesting questions involve the nature of consciousness and how generally it permeates all of creation. Maybe our ongoing encounter with the White Sasquatch has something to do with this mystery. The interpenetration of our inner and outer worlds, is, I think, the prime quality of man's experience of the sacred. The synchronistic events, the apparent communications, Donna's feeling of connection, even my own dreams about the creature – when coupled with the concrete evidence, the broken tree, the boulder striking the water –seem, I admit, sacred or otherworldly. Maybe therein lies the power of this creature who is so like us and yet so different. He connects our inner and outer worlds, the human and the non-human realms. If you must seek him out, do not invade the forest or set traps like a hunter. Walk quietly in the woods. Listen to the wind and the songs of birds. Maybe you will find a footprint or a broken tree. Maybe you will just find the mystery in your own heart.

November 2015

November 14

During the last week in October, Donna returned to Gate 3A by herself for the first time since she had hiked there in the years before I knew her. She was troubled by the signs of recent logging, deep ruts in the road, and rocks churned up out of the ground, so she did not stay long. She returned the next day and followed the path farther down to the boulder that marked the place from which she had looked into the forest and seen the tall white figure walking. She went a short way past, then turned around and was stunned by what she saw. Across the trail down which she had just walked lay a small maple tree, its red autumn leaves blazing in the afternoon sun. How could she have missed such a sign, walking as she was into the realm of the White Sasquatch? And yet, there had been no sound of a tree falling. It seemed to her that the fallen maple, vibrant with color, had just appeared there in an instant, like an enormous autumn bouquet. A gift? A boundary marker? To keep her in, not out? Donna had come to leave a gift, but she did not expect one in return. Her gift was a necklace, a turquoise heart pendant just like one she had given to her youngest daughter just before her daughter left for France. It still hung around Donna's neck as she stared at the little fallen maple.

She walked about fifty yards through that brushy, logged-over area into the edge of the forest where she had seen Luke. She chose a recognizable cluster of trees and knelt down behind the largest one. She took the pendant off and buried it under the leaves behind the trunk. Only a bit of the black string remained visible. She walked back out to the path, took some pictures of the "fallen" tree, then left.

When she returned the following week, the pendant was gone. She scratched around behind the tree for a few minutes, but it was nowhere to be found. She called me that night and told me this strange story, and the following day I went back with her to the trail. The tree was still there though its leaves had faded from the bright red I saw in her photos. I could not imagine how, walking by herself, nervously watchful, she could have missed such a sign on her first pass. She took me to that cluster of trees and again got down on her knees and dug around through the leaves and forest litter. Nothing was there. Could I possibly imagine all of this as some odd fabrication, her tenaciously clinging to a wondrous chapter in our lives that was receding into the past? I don't really know what to believe, but knowing Donna as I do, I find this the least likely of explanations. Besides, she always wore that necklace, and I had not seen it now since that day she says she left it beneath the tree. It was a kind of talisman, a prayer for the safety of her children and those she loved, and now she had left it as an offering to the White Sasquatch.

For several weeks, as I've tried to imagine a title for this book, the word "convergence" has lodged in my mind like an unexpected guest. What did this word have to do with our story about an improbable being in a regenerated wilderness?

Con-verge: a prefix, "con," meaning "against" and "verge," an old word for limit, edge or border; together, they form a modern verb expressing a flowing together as when two streams merge to form a river.

As our encounter with Luke evolved, Donna and I were pushed against the borders of our own identities and the limits of our understanding. We discovered the parts of ourselves that didn't seem to fit together properly, but we continued on, pursuing the mystery that had become a refuge from our daily struggles. Maybe mystery, the magic of our own improbable existence, is what we all need to make those daily struggles worthwhile, to be fully human, or, should I say, fully conscious. Maybe this very fascination with the unknown is what drew Luke to Donna…

I believe now that during this protracted encounter, our characters and world views converged with the mind of a human cousin whose formidable intelligence may always remain at some level unknowable, who perceives details in our physical environment that we have never known. Luke and his tribe most likely see things we cannot see and hear sounds we cannot hear. Maybe this is the key to their elusiveness. Yet, I am sure that we and Luke have communicated through the prisms of our separate realities. He and I converged on that path with Donna. Through her eyes, I saw him gliding behind the trees and immediately knew him to be real. I could feel his presence like the air against my skin. He did not care about being seen by Donna. He already knew her. She was the golden-haired smiling woman in the little house at the other end of the power lines, an intermediary between his forest and the dangerous realms beyond.

Perhaps I would never know him the way she did. Still, like her, I could accept the redeeming mystery each of our kinds represent to the other.

About the Author

John Coster is a performing singer and instrumentalist best known for his original songs and innovative treatments of Celtic-based traditional music. *The Boston Globe* has referred to John as a "song writer of unusual eloquence and sensitivity." He has a BA from Harvard University where he studied English Literature, Anthropology, and History. He pursued further studies in Psychology and the History of Religion at the Hartford Seminary Foundation and is presently doing research for a book about the lives of some of his ancestors who were prominent figures in the American Revolution. John is a longtime resident of the Pioneer Valley in western Massachusetts where he spends much of his free time hiking and exploring the abundant forests of the region.

He can be reached at john.medicineb@gmail.com. John's website is www.johncostermusic.com.

45319036R00083

Made in the USA
San Bernardino, CA
05 February 2017